HOME CHIC

Translated from the French
by Louise Rogers Lalaurie
Design: Noémie Levain
Copyediting: Lindsay Porter
Typesetting: Gravemaker+Scott
Proofreading: Nicole Foster
Color Separation: Frédéric Claudel, Paris
Printed in Slovakia by TBB, a.s.

Originally published in French as *Home*
© Flammarion, S.A., Paris, 2012

English-language edition
© Flammarion, S.A., Paris, 2013

editions.flammarion.com

13 14 15 3 2 1

ISBN: 978-2-08-020141-6

Dépôt légal: 04/2013

india mahdavi

with soline delos

Home CHic

decorating with style

Flammarion

introduction

At a dinner party, the trouble with being an interior designer—
which is almost as bad as being a doctor—is that other guests
can't resist asking for advice. "Oh! You're a doctor? Listen, I
have this chronic back pain. . . ." Or, in my case, "So you're India
Mahdavi? We've been thinking about redoing our living room,
and we'd love to know what you think."

That's why I wrote this straightforward guide, offering clear
explanations—illustrated with photographs and drawings—to
answer the questions we all ask about our apartment or home
interiors. Here are my guiding principles and easy tips for
creating a sublime home: you can follow my rules, break them,
or pick your favorites and combine them with your own taste and
color schemes. The choice is yours!

However big or small your space, or your budget, this book
will help your Home Sweet Home look sweeter than ever. It's just
as important to feel comfortable at home as it is "in your own
skin." Home really is where the heart is. I hope you'll find what
you're looking for in the pages of my "homemade" book—I wrote
it at home, *chez moi*, but I was thinking first and foremost about
chez vous.

contents

5   introduction

01 "home" at first sight

10   getting around
12   should it stay, or should it go?
14   the big three
16   a whiter shade of pale
18   the best-laid plans
20   follow your eye
22   in the picture

02 the beauty in the beast

32   rise to new heights
34   rear windows
36   afraid of the dark?
38   in search of lost space
40   well grounded

03 a space of my own

44   making an entrance
48   room for living
52   *bon appetit!*
56   do not disturb, it's time for bed
60   sweet dreams, little one!
62   what's cooking?
68   bathing beauty
72   the smallest room

04 mix to the max

78   the style mix
86   the marriage of venus and mars
104   cheap and cheerful vs. luxury chic

05 **successful accessories**

110   coffee tables
112   curtains and shades
116   lamps
120   rugs

06 **quick fixes**

124   sell it, move it, replace it
126   reincarnation

07 **hip to be square**

134   go green
136   *la vie en rose*
138   out of the closet
140   so kitsch!

08 **my city guide**

144   Beirut
148   Bombay (Mumbai)
150   Istanbul
152   Cape Town
156   Lisbon
158   London
161   Mexico City
164   Los Angeles
166   Milan
168   New York
174   Paris
186   Rio de Janeiro
190   my favorite online addresses
192   … and Siwa

01 "home" at first sight

This time it's the real deal: you've only just met, but you know you're made for each other. And like partners in love, you and your new living space will soon come down from Cloud Nine, well aware of the compromises you need to make if it's going to last. In which case, all the time (and money) you can spare will be well spent. So while you apply that fresh coat of the "right" white, think about getting rid of unnecessary doors, too. Shift those awkward radiators, replace ugly light switches, eliminate alcoves you really don't need. And above all, beware of "temporary" solutions that you know, deep down, will become permanent. Follow my list of top tips to help make the most of your space.

getting around

Ease of circulation is all-important in an apartment, and the easier it is to move around, the bigger your home will feel. Follow my pointers to open up your space, eliminate superfluous features, and create a home with comfortable living areas that are easy on the eye.
And breathe. . . .

Remove unnecessary doors between the living room and the dining room, between the living room and the hall: in short, remove all the doors you're unlikely ever to close. The aim is to create perspectives, to make it easier to move around, and to open up the available space as much as possible.

Remove suspended (dropped) ceilings. This will add height and has the additional advantage of getting rid of those inevitable recessed spotlights—they belong in the kitchen and bathroom, and nowhere else! Ceiling spots cast an unattractive, impersonal light, and no one wants to feel like they're living in a shopping mall.

Move awkwardly placed radiators. There will always be a radiator just where you want to put your sofa, a desk, or another large piece of furniture. Allow yourself a small budget (and a reputable handyman) to move it. Ideally, (re)locate your radiator underneath a window or behind your curtains. If that's not possible, build a narrow shelf directly above it—perfect for objects and photographs.

Choose a unified floor treatment (plain fitted carpet, sisal, or parquet) for all rooms except for the bathroom and kitchen. This will help create a more fluid space, especially in small apartments.

no!

. . . to overdesigned plastic light switches with integral night-lights—the kind you expect to see in an office, but never at home. Replace them with plated metal ones: they are more expensive, but like your treasured Louboutins, they last a lifetime, and they go with everything. And if retro light switches account for the last pennies of your budget, don't worry about those white plastic electric plugs: they will pass unnoticed, especially on white walls.

should it stay, or should it go?

Governed by taste or by necessity, initial decisions on what stays or goes are all-important. In an old apartment oozing period charm, it can be difficult to choose between features that are genuinely attractive and others that clutter or dominate the space, however "historic." Genuine cachet or overpowering and intrusive?

Just follow these simple rules:

That open fireplace can go! It may be in an awkward spot, it may not be usable. Pull it out and sell it, no regrets! If you like the feature but hate your chimneypiece, try some *trompe-l'oeil* marbling for the surround, paint the hearth black, and install a pair of attractive iron firedogs from your local antiques market. (Be persistent—they aren't always easy to come by.)

Remove low paneling or wainscoting. This will lighten up your wall space and make way for a picture rail from which to hang your treasured art collection.

Cover misplaced alcove niches—between two windows, for example. Over time, you will find these become the first and only thing you see in a room, like an unwelcome pimple on the nose! If the niche is small enough, you may be able to hide it behind a picture.

Conceal exposed stonework with a coat of plaster. Unless you're moving into a château or a rustic farmhouse, or you just *love* that "country gastro-pub" look, plaster over that stonework.

Cover terra-cotta tiles with carpet, because I *so* regret not following my own advice *chez moi*.

Paint your exposed beams white. Ignore your realtor's horrified look, exposed beams darken a room dreadfully, not to mention their extremely bad *feng shui*. Try going all the way and painting the ceiling in between the beams blue or yellow. You can even paint the beams different colors—like French contemporary art star Daniel Buren in his Paris studio.

the big three

There's no getting away from it—sooner or later, you will have to remodel a kitchen, camouflage bathroom tiles, or find space for the dressing room of your dreams. Keep calm and focus on finding the right solution.

Bathrooms

Just because your bathroom tiling is a throwback to a past era, with a flower on every square, doesn't mean you have to change it! Introduce some strong statements—a shower curtain covered with a bold textile, an outsize mirror, a collection of photographs around the washbasin, and you'll hardly notice the tiles, and save on an expensive replacement job to boot.

Kitchens

There are only two options, in my opinion, for anyone looking to create a new kitchen from scratch, or transform their existing units: (1) IKEA (where else?), and their Abstrakt range (my favorite) in glossy red or silver-gray lacquer, a stylish change from the conventional white; (2) ask a carpenter to make new doors only and paint them with the gloss color of your choice.

In both cases, personalize your doors with quirky handles or doorknobs picked up at your local flea market or hardware store (one of my favorites is La Quincaillerie on the Boulevard Saint-Germain, in Paris).

Dressing rooms

All fashionistas dream of having their very own dressing space: it's one room that's guaranteed to put you in a good mood every morning. The next best thing (if your bedroom space permits) is wall-to-wall, floor-to-ceiling fitted storage (now you're glad you moved that awkward radiator). The best budget option is IKEA's Stolmen range, tucked behind a sweeping velvet drape. For custom-built solutions, ask your handyman to install floor-to-ceiling shelves, unless you have plaster cornices, in which case align the wardrobe to the top of your bedroom door.

a whiter shade of pale

Color is purely and simply a matter of taste, but mistakes can be made, and the subtleties of taupe, gray, and every shade of white need careful consideration. So here are the rules for all my girlfriends who ask, every time they move, "Which white should I use for my new apartment?"

01 Chalk white

The whitest white. Use it when you don't want any hint of color on your walls. It's perfect for beachfront properties—and it was my white of choice for the Monte-Carlo Beach hotel, in Monaco. It works perfectly with bold motifs and fresh, vibrant colors.

02 Plaster white

Very slightly "aged." I created this color for people who, like me, love the understated charm of slightly faded paintwork. Use it for walls, in combination with chalk white for the ceiling and moldings: this is the ideal combination for a "classic" interior. For a more contemporary look, use the same white (either chalk white or plaster white) on walls, ceiling, and moldings alike.

03 Pale gray

For a more urban, metropolitan, masculine look.

04 Warm beige

Perfect for collectors: nothing displays your artworks better than this. Use it and abuse it. (See p. 22.)

QUICK TIP
Keep strong colors for small spaces. In a larger room, use color on one wall only, preferably on the wall that is perpendicular to the windows.

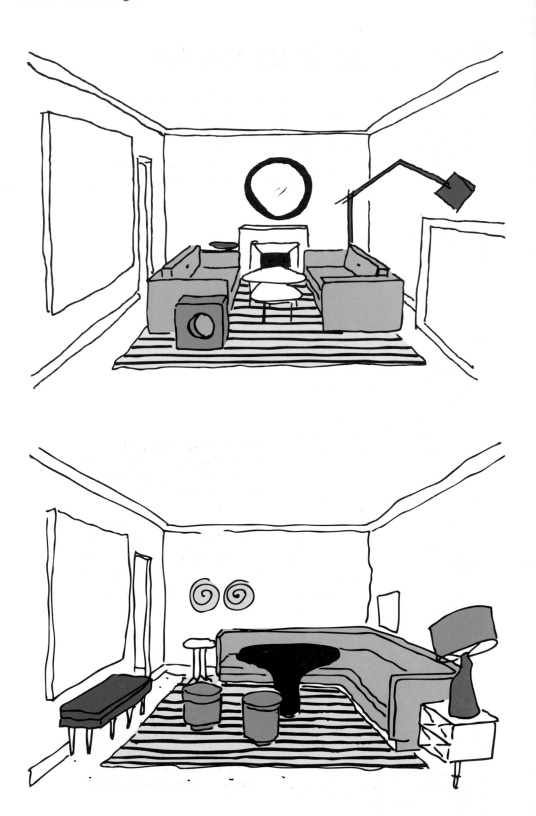

the best-laid plans

You've taken out doors, repainted, and moved radiators. Now it's time to furnish your space. Placing your sofa and other pieces may seem easy, but often it's the most complicated part of the decorating process. Finding the perfect place for your sofa can take time, but the good news is that it's easier to move than a partition wall.

Mark out your floor plan with colored tape. This is my favorite trick when I'm planning a new layout. It's a quick and easy way to find out if your arrangement of sofas and coffee tables, or that new partition wall, will really work.

Use common-sense rules to position your sofa, whether next to the fireplace or facing an attractive view. If in doubt, try moving a chair around your room until you find a spot that feels "just right." And remember, if no one ever plops down on your sofa, it's in the wrong place!

Avoid that "showroom" look. Choose a less conventional layout for your furniture. Anchor the room with a strong statement (two sofas and a coffee table, for example), then "deconstruct" the rest of the space—place a desk between two windows, put a bookcase or sofa in one corner, add a second coffee table or a chaise longue. Make the most of quirky, non-essential but charming pieces in unlikely settings, such as in front of a window or a bookcase. They add tons of personality to an interior, and your friends will love them.

There's a place for everything. Every piece of furniture has a spot just made for it, somewhere in your home. The best way to discover it is through trial and error: you'll know immediately when you've found the right place. (Hearing yourself say "Why didn't I think of putting it there before?" is a good sign.)

GOLDEN RULE
To see if your arrangement really works, take a photograph: a room's strong points and faults are far more obvious when captured on film than when viewed with the naked eye.

follow your eye

Allow your eye to wander naturally over your space: you'll find your gaze is drawn beyond the first object you see in the foreground, to a second piece further away, a third in the background, and so on. It's vital to organize your home around these natural perspectives, so that each new discovery—a living room, a bathroom, or a hallway— becomes a visual treat. Take care over each room's visual "hook," such as an armchair, a picture, a wall light, a sculptural lamp, or a colored wall.

Add extra interest to passageways and perspectives, such as a well-placed drawing, a place to sit, a wall light, or all three at once!

in the picture

Hooks and hammer at the ready, it's time to hang your pictures. This all-important, penultimate stage (before the final "styling") is too often neglected, but it's important to get it right: the works of art on your wall are the first thing anyone sees when they enter a room. Unsure where to bang in that nail? Follow these basic rules, for guaranteed success. And watch your fingers!

Assemble your artwork, whether photographs, drawings, or sculptures, into miniature "worlds." Hang them on the wall, or place them on the mantel or a piece of furniture to create an imaginative escape.

Offbeat combinations are the antidote to boredom (in life, and on your living-room wall!). Display a painting against bold, patterned wallpaper, or on a shelf in your bookcase; hang a picture off-center on a wall, or on a door (provided it stays open all the time, like mine, masking a radiator). You can even try placing one on the floor. *But try only one of these—a single, strong statement is the key!*

Grouped picture frames are great, but stick to a unified format.

Display big pictures with other big pictures, and small to medium-sized frames together, no more than 2 inches (5 cm) apart. Hang them in an entrance, a hallway, the bathroom—wherever they can be seen and enjoyed up close.

When you hang a picture on a wall, you also create a void around it.
The empty space should offset the picture, or vice versa, but if the two are competing for your attention, think again.

GOLDEN RULE
Anchor pictures by placing
them no more than
10–12 inches (25–30 cm)
above a piece of furniture
(sofas included).

QUICK TIP
If, like me, you hang your pictures
by eye (no tape measure,
no carpenter's level), you'll
find yourself filling in those
annoying misplaced nail-holes
from time to time. Arm yourself
with a tube of Spackle and
a spatula to cover your tracks.
A dab of gouache from your
children's paint-box will finish
the job on colored walls.

02 the beauty in the beast

We all have our strengths, plus other features we try to downplay. The same applies at home! To balance out your bottom half, you accentuate your height and waistline, right? Or maybe you emphasize your eyes to draw attention away from a big nose. At home, the principle is exactly the same: encourage the eye to ignore low ceilings, dark rooms, or a depressing outlook. Here's how.

rise to new heights

A low ceiling has the effect of shrinking your living space. To compensate, highlight the walls and floor, with interesting patterns and character.

Choose pale shades, and paint your walls and ceiling the same color to blend the transition between the two. Alternatively, do the complete opposite: go for a white ceiling, and a richly patterned wallpaper (but avoid overly large motifs).

Draw attention to your floor with a graphic, patterned carpet *à la* David Hicks. This is the best way to direct your eye away from the ceiling.

Don't be afraid to use oversized furniture. The resulting "optical illusion" is highly effective.

Add vertical shapes and patterns. Floor lamps, tall bookcases, full-length curtains—use anything to create an impression of height. This includes doors: emphasize their verticality by adding 1940s-style moldings (buy them ready-made or ask a cabinetmaker to make some).

rear windows

When your window overlooks a depressing apartment block or a wall four yards away, there's only one solution: camouflage the view, but remember to let in as much light as possible. Light falls from above, so concentrate on the lower section of your window, and use your imagination!

Place an attractive pair of chairs, or a big, colorful armchair (see my tip about offbeat items in section 01, p.19) in front of the window.

Add fine cotton or linen curtains at half-height across the window. These will allow the light in, but block the view.

Find a pretty, folding screen from your local flea market and place it in front of the window—it should reach no more than halfway up. Add patterned curtains to either side. (This is my solution at home, to hide the huge neon sign across the street.)

GOLDEN RULE
If an imperfection jumps out at you in a room, introduce a bold object or an interesting piece of furniture to draw attention elsewhere.

afraid of the dark?

The obvious solutions are not always the best: low furniture should be banned from rooms with low ceilings, and we should never assume that a dark room must be painted white. Tackle a room's shortcomings head-on, and don't try to pretend they don't exist.

Charcoal gray walls in a dark room? Of course. Even if you paint it white, the room will never be light. Here, an accident in my study is a perfect example.

Choose objects and furniture with bright, reflective surfaces (glossy paint, lacquer, Plexiglass), plus velvety fabrics to reflect and capture the light.

Bring back your old halogen lamp, to cast light up onto the ceiling. (NB: permission is granted *only* in these exceptional circumstances.)

It's okay to leave your lights on, even during the day.

yes! . . . to a wall of mirrors, which is making a big comeback at the moment. Or, prop a large mirror against one wall—either option will capture and reflect as much light as possible. This works well in every room—living rooms, hallways, dining rooms. But remember to take each space on a case-by-case basis!

in search of lost space

To me, there is no such thing as "wasted space." On the contrary, long corridors, large hallways, and rooms with no specific purpose are what allows a home to breathe, giving it a welcoming, relaxed, luxurious feel, and adding charm and personality.

A simple trick to "square up" an irregularly shaped room: paint one of the walls (but not the awkwardly shaped one) in a strong color.

Transform a long corridor or entrance hall into a portrait gallery. You can either hang your pictures or sit them on the floor, propped against the wall. This is an ideal way to display family photographs— maximum size 20 × 25 inches (50 × 60 cm)—provided you choose only the very best shots! Choose white, natural oak, black, or steel frames, but avoid dark wooden frames which can look dated and unsophisticated.

Emphasize your staircase with bold wallpaper, wall lights, and a graphic, patterned stair carpet.

GOLDEN RULE
Don't despair about that long corridor, oversized entrance hall, or odd-shaped room: "awkward" areas like these can become valuable breathing spaces, or focal points for objects and pictures. Forget practicalities— use your imagination!

well grounded

My Top Three unattractive floors: (1) over-varnished, rust-orange parquet or cheap laminate flooring; (2) "smoked" tile; and (3) fake "rustic" stone paving. If you have one or more of these, you are hereby authorized to try at least one of my camouflage solutions below!

Solution no. 1 (my favorite): if your parquet floor or tiles are irreparably awful, use a **100-percent wool, cotton, or linen fitted carpet** throughout (Hartley & Tissier Ltd of Paris get my vote), or a more affordable wool-polyester version. Once your furniture is in place, it's almost impossible to tell the difference.

Solution no. 2 is every bit as attractive, but for parquet or cement floors only: **apply a coat of floor paint in all rooms, to unify your space**. Choose pale neutrals like plaster white, beige, pale gray, or taupe; or dark shades of black, navy blue, or charcoal gray, but *never* "imitation wood."

Try combinations of different colors, too: white and gray, black and ivory, rose-pink and chestnut. This is a great way to add real character to your floor—but tends to work best in beachside or country homes.

no!

. . . to hollow-sounding, cheap laminate flooring.

. . . to tinted gloss varnish for your parquet (the colors are too boring). Choose a tinted matt varnish or wax instead, or a specialist floor paint in a satin or high-gloss finish. Make sure you select an eco-friendly formula.

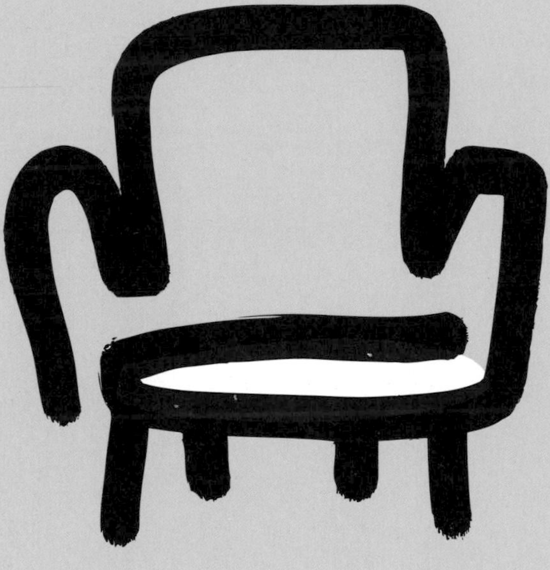

03 a space of my own

There's nothing worse than a cold, empty dining room, a clinical kitchen, or a "showroom" living room. Each room in your home should feel comfortable, lived-in, alive (with just the right amount of organized disorder), and, above all, unique. Read on for my dos and don'ts to give your space that extra touch of personality.

INSTALL A SOFA OR A LARGE ARMCHAIR.
Even if you never sit in it, it will add a note of visual
comfort, making a hall feel lived-in, and replacing
the inevitable coatrack.

IF YOU HAVE A LARGE ENTRANCE HALL,
GIVE IT MULTIPLE FUNCTIONS:
a hallway-cum-library, a hallway-cum-office,
or a hallway-cum-dining room. Above all,
avoid the hallway-cum-storeroom.
This is *not* a welcoming look.

making an entrance

You never get a second chance to make a first impression, as the old saying goes, yet all too often we neglect the impact of the first room we see after stepping through the front door. Big or small, your hallway is your first chance to make a strong style statement, and extend an irresistible invitation to *come on in*.

A HUMOROUS TOUCH WILL BRING A SMILE TO YOUR GUESTS' FACES!

YOUR FRONT DOOR MAY NOT BE YOUR HALLWAY'S BEST FEATURE. Hide it behind a thick velvet or linen drape. This provides insulation against the cold and outside noise, too.

Opt for neutral shades of beige,
taupe, and gray: all the sober
elegance and chic of a 1930s interior.

no!
. . . to big, central chandeliers or ceiling lamps. So passé. Avoid them in your hallway, and everywhere else. Ceiling suspensions should hang in corners if they hang at all.

Avoid the unholy trinity (console table + mirror + bunch of flowers). Choose an unusual, asymmetric console, and a bold, statement wall lamp instead.

IF YOU HAVE ROOM, CREATE SEVERAL DIFFERENT SPACES IN YOUR LIVING AREA. DON'T BE AFRAID TO "CLUTTER"— YOUR ROOM WILL COME TO LIFE!

no!

. . . to the TV in the middle of the bookshelves in the living room. A flat screen is not a treasured decorative object.

NOTHING BEATS A PAIR OF SOFAS PLACED FACE-TO-FACE: (1) they add visual structure to a room, and (2) they make a convivial conversation space. But too much symmetry can be tedious: break it up with a variety of coffee tables and lamps.

The aim is to avoid the classic, 100-percent symmetrical look (a pair of identical table lamps on two identical coffee tables on either side of a pair of sofas, or either side of the fireplace)— bourgeois "taste" at its worst.

room for living

Your living room should be, well, the liveliest room in your home. That sterile "showroom" look is out of the question. The acid test? If you enjoy entertaining all the neighbors here on a cozy Sunday evening (like me!) just as much as you love kicking back here alone and surfing on your iPad.

A RUG BETWEEN TWO SOFAS: the indispensable accessory that anchors your conversation space.

INSTANT CHIC: My trademark Bishop stool in turquoise, pink, yellow, or gold is guaranteed to liven up any space. Add a scattering of bold, patterned cushions, and a throw, or a "fur" for the sofa. These three simple accessories will lift the mood of any interior.

I use my chaise longue to display striking, graphic objects like chess sets, or this backgammon board, adding pattern and interest to a plain black surface.

no!

. . . to family photos in silver frames on a round table complete with table cloth. Déjà vu.

GOLDEN RULE
Big sofas make small rooms seem bigger, while several small sofas will liven up a large room, giving a warm, friendly feel.

USE SIDE TABLES TO PUNCTUATE YOUR SPACE. Bright colors and ceramic tops are ideal. The smallest pieces of furniture can make big statements when chosen for their boldness.

no!

. . . to fragrant candles in
the dining room. They will
clash with the aroma of
your roast chicken and thyme.

Banquette seating is a great idea if,
like mine, your dining table is
in the corner of the room.

AN EMPTY TABLE IS LIKE A BLANK WALL:
DRESS IT UP! Add a bowl full of seasonal fruit,
four piles of coffee-table books (all at different
heights), or a small decorative sculpture.

bon appetit!

Avoid "empty dining-room syndrome" (your ironing board will spend more time in there than you). Bring it to life with an off-center table (as here), for a less conventional feel. Or double up (as in the hallway) by creating a dining room-cum-library or study. The choice is yours!

WHAT SHAPE FOR THE TABLE? Rectangular or oval if you prefer a large table (always a good idea in a small room); small or medium-sized tables should be round or square.

no!

... to central ceiling lights, guaranteed to age your guests a decade each.

TWO CHOICES FOR CHAIRS: Boho chic with mismatched shapes picked up at your local flea market (buy them in pairs, to avoid the "junk shop" look). Or designer chic, with a complete set by a signature name, like my favorite Osso chairs by the Bouroullec brothers, or pieces by Friso Kamer (the Netherlands' answer to Jean Prouvé). Track them on eBay, or at vintage antiques fairs.

Avoid the "cafeteria look," with chairs neatly tucked in under your table. Place them around the room, in pairs—against one wall, in front of a window, or on either side of the table. Use them to display a pile of art books, or a treasured decorative object.

yes!

. . . to mix-and-match tableware (this works very well for dinner guests, too). I collect stylish plates, soup bowls, salad bowls, and glasses on my travels. Every dinner table is a cheerful mix of memories from Egypt, Morocco, Mexico, Mongolia, Iran, South Africa, England, and France. In perfect harmony, of course!

MAKE YOUR BED THE STAR OF THE SHOW. Give it pride of place, facing the fireplace, or a window (if you have a great view). Treat yourself to the ultimate in comfort: I test my mattresses in the bedding department at the local department store. Or try a Contour mattress with a mattress topper from Tempur-Pedic (www.tempurpedic.com).

A COLORFUL WOOL OR CASHMERE THROW adds instant comfort and softness, like your favorite pashmina shawl.

THE RIGHT HEIGHT FOR YOUR BED is 24–28 inches (60–65 cm) from the floor, leaving plenty of room to slip your gym mat and weights underneath, out of sight.

do not disturb, it's time for bed

Your bedroom is the most intimate, personal space in your home: it's where you sleep, dream, love.... And since we spend almost half of our lives here, it's worth taking the time to personalize the decor. No one wants to go to sleep in a soulless hotel.

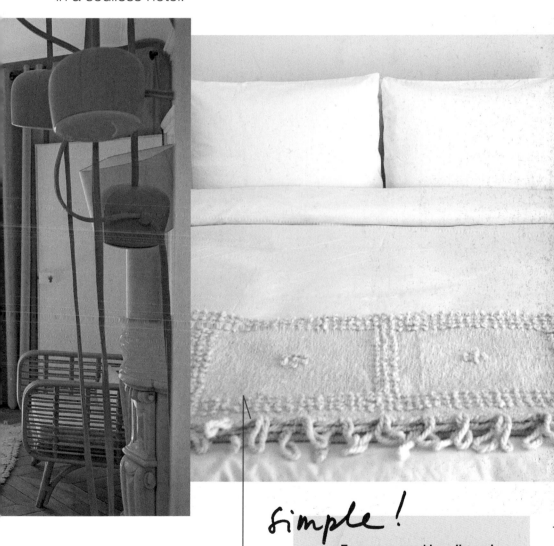

WHITE IS THE ESSENTIAL COLOR FOR SHEETS, duvet covers, and pillowcases: instant chic, with the added touch of an ethnic, natural cream wool throw (your whites will look even whiter).

simple!

For an unusual headboard, use a fine, woven wool rug (have it cleaned first), or a bold, colorful Suzani textile from Uzbekistan.

no!

...to ceiling lights over the bed—the most un-sexy lighting possible.

no!

...to matching headboards and divan covers, the decorating equivalent of the ultimate fashion *faux pas*—matching shoes and handbag. *Never* a good look.

REMEMBER THE CORRECT FORMULA FOR BEDSIDE LAMPS AND TABLES: if your tables are a pair, use mismatched lamps (40-watt bulbs are best), and vice versa.

Your bedroom is THE place
for family photos.

YES TO A BEDROOM ARMCHAIR—
essential for that home pedicure,
or as a place to throw your clothes.
But no to footboards at the bottom
of the bed, laundry baskets, "valet"
stands, and concealed lighting
in the curtain pelmet. This is not
a hotel!

TV OR NOT TV? Bedroom TVs are
admissible (but not compulsory),
provided they don't make their presence
felt. Giant screens are *out*: place your
small flat-screen on the chimneypiece
or a low console table.

Beautiful, framed photographs are much more fun than tattered posters.

CHOOSE A FUN COATRACK, like this one from Gervasoni. Hang it with costume headdresses and hats: instant decoration, and perfect for children's birthday parties or Halloween!

PAINT ONE WALL IN FOUR DIFFERENT-COLORED SECTIONS (I did this in my son's bedroom), or one strong color: this is a great way to (visually) absorb the mess in children's rooms.

simple!

Use wicker baskets for storage: the natural material balances your children's plastic toys.

sweet dreams, little one!

Your children's bedrooms are every bit as important as your own. Throw convention to the wind! (1) Primary colors and cheap plastic furniture are *not* compulsory. (2) Children don't always destroy everything, and the prettier their furniture, the less likely they are to wreck it.

COLORED BLACKBOARD PAINT ON THE WALLS is a great way to give free rein to their budding artistic talents (and infinitely preferable to your living-room wall).

AVOID CHILD-SIZED DESKS: CHOOSE A VINTAGE MODEL from your local flea market, and protect it with a glass top. They'll take it with them when they move out!

Combine recessed lighting with stylish pendant lights; the best way to give your kitchen a strong personality.

A VELVET SCREEN, BLACK-AND-WHITE PHOTOGRAPHS, A TABLE LAMP: REMEMBER, YOUR KITCHEN IS A "LIVING ROOM," TOO!

A REAL KITCHEN TABLE IS ESSENTIAL. There's nothing nicer than a cozy kitchen supper for two or ten! Choose a colorful model with an unusual shape: vintage yellow Formica from a vintage dealer, for example, or a bold geometric design. Your kitchen table can double as a home office: if you like eating here, you'll like working here, too (but avoid the temptation to snack).

what's cooking?

We spend far more time in the kitchen than the dining room: this is the place for family lunches, children's dinners, late-night suppers. No one wants a frigid, minimalist laboratory at the heart of their home. A kitchen should be functional, of course, but friendly and welcoming, too.

no!

... to ugly, plastic trash cans, which are often too small. Replace with a large, metal model. Your garbage pail deserves as much care as your recycling.

MISMATCHED SEATING IS INFORMAL, FUN, and a great excuse to bring out those chairs and stools you haven't used for years!

MY KITCHEN IS ALSO WHERE
I DISPLAY STYLISH POSTCARDS
AND INVITATIONS.

PUT A TABLE LAMP
ON YOUR KITCHEN TABLE.
Hardly anyone thinks to
do this, but it can change
the mealtime atmosphere,
casting a soft, sexy light.

yes!
 A big fruit platter, or fresh
aromatic herbs growing in a
pot, will perfume your kitchen
far more effectively than a
"meadow" aerosol spray.

TRY REPLACING YOUR SURGICAL STEEL SPLASHBOARD with something more decorative. Framed pictures attract the eye away from your hotplates and the (inevitable) surrounding clutter (but make sure they're at a safe distance from sources of heat!).

KEEP YOUR UTENSILS HANDY IN BIG CLAY POTS, vintage carafes, or solid wooden containers. Practical and decorative, if you lack drawer space.

AN OPEN-PLAN KITCHEN IS IDEAL FOR SMALL APARTMENTS, allowing you to expand your kitchen and living room all at once! Hide it away when not in use behind a set of sliding doors, or choose a stylish, lacquered gloss finish (IKEA, of course): the result is simultaneously eye-catching and discreet. In both cases, *keep it neat and tidy*.

Choose bold, plain-colored
cabinets and a graphic floor pattern
for a dynamic effect.

The best place for your "wardrobe wall": between the bathroom and your bedroom.

A FUR RUG IN THE BATHROOM? Yes! You can even use it as a bath mat, provided you place a small cotton towel on top. Fun fur rugs are welcome, too, of course—the softer they are underfoot, the better.

bathing beauty

I'm not afraid of water! Velvet drapes, treasured objects, black-and-white photographs, fur rugs, even a matching furry ottoman—very Las Vegas chic—transform my bathroom into a luxurious space for serious pampering.

A VINTAGE CHAIR, A COZY ARMCHAIR—your bathroom is a boudoir, too.

My "mini-museum" for visual interest above the bathtub!

Bath towels should be white, fluffy, and soft. Just like the plush towels at Claridge's in London or the Hôtel Thoumieux in Paris!

no!

. . . to open boxes of tissues, cotton buds, or cotton balls on display. Keep them out of sight, in attractive, closed containers.

AN UNUSUALLY SHAPED MIRROR, OR A VINTAGE FIND from your local flea market will add loads of cachet. Or try a mirror wall.

Yes to bathroom wallpaper, provided your room is well ventilated, or has a window.

THE GOLDEN RULE FOR PERFECT BATHROOM LIGHTING: lamps at face height, from the front or side, combined with ceiling lights, as here at the Monte-Carlo Beach hotel.

yes!
... to heated towel rails.
A warm towel is a wonderful treat, even in summer.

Bathroom colors should aim to brighten your morning (especially in winter) and put you in a good mood. Don't be afraid to use yellow, pink, or turquoise (the latter works best in beachside settings) but avoid green—that reflected "corpse" complexion is not a good look.

no!

. . . to pink, blue, patterned, or black toilet paper. The only way is white. No to fragrant toilet paper and synthetic aerosol fragrances, too. Use an eau de toilette spray from your favorite perfumer.

CHOOSE SILVER TILE for a hip, nightclub look.

no!

. . . to cleaning products and dry, tattered sponges lurking "out of sight" behind the toilet. These are instant style killers. My golden rule: cleaning products and equipment *always* live in the cleaning cupboard!

the smallest room

Just because the door is permanently closed, don't neglect the throne room behind it! Your bathroom can be a visually sumptuous, luxurious retreat. Think big, bold, and beautiful.

FILL THE SHELVES WITH QUICK, EASY READS. I keep my thesaurus, dictionaries, and old reference books here, plus a few "specialist" volumes, like Henry Miller's *The Books in My Life*, which has a section on "Reading in the Toilet."

CHOOSE FLORAL WALLPAPER or gloss paint in fresh, bright colors, for that essential touch of sophistication.

simple!

Turn the smallest room into a family snapshot gallery. No need for frames—colored pins are great!

IF YOUR BATHROOM IS BIG ENOUGH, CONCEAL THE "THRONE," behind a folding screen or a half-height partition wall. If you're starting from scratch, avoid placing the toilet just opposite the door.

WICKER BASKETS MAKE THE BEST BATHROOM WASTEBASKETS. They're a stylish, practical alternative to fiddly toilet roll holders, too.

AVOID PRINTED, PATTERNED, LEOPARD-SKIN, FLORAL, AND SEASHELL TOILET SEATS. White, black, or natural wood only.

yes!
... to piles of (carefully selected) magazines on the floor, for a dash of instant chic. My recommendations? *Vanity Fair* and *The New Yorker*, plus French *Vogue* and *Elle*, for that cosmopolitan touch.

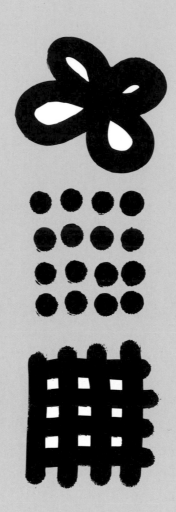

04 mix to the max

With interiors as with fashion, mixing it up is the key to a truly individual look.

Take a page out of my style book, and be bold! Mix vintage with contemporary, cheap and cheerful with luxury chic, floral and geometric motifs, bright colors and neutrals, "warm" and "cold" materials. It's all a question of harmony and balance between your home's masculine and feminine sides—this is the key to a successful, error-free combination.

the style mix

The furniture and objects you collect over the years

speak volumes about your personality, your history,

the people and things you love most, and the person

you are. That unique, individual mix is the key to

a truly stylish, "living" interior. Don't hide it, flaunt it!

Follow the golden rule for a successful, eclectic mix: **diverse styles, periods, fabrics, and materials should unite around a common theme**, as here at the Connaught, in London's Mayfair. A graphic carpet *à la* David Hicks is associated with English velvet-upholstered armchairs, pieces from my own furniture collection, classic "English club" paneling, and medallion portraits by British artist Julian Opie.

Objects, materials, and motifs come together on a plant theme with leafy print cushions and wallpaper, a fabulous tree screen, and bamboo furniture—the guest of honor in this conservatory-style living room.

Avoid performing the stylistic splits! If in doubt, **stick to objects and furniture from no more than three different decades—** this simple tip is virtually infallible. Here, 1960s ceramic lamps are teamed with my signature Bishop stools and a 1970s Maria Pergay bed.

the marriage
of venus and mars

We're always being told to get in touch with our masculine (or feminine) side. I recommend trying this at home, too. A balance of male/female elements in a room creates perfect harmony. Learn to tell the difference, in materials, colors, shapes, and prints. Experiment with a Prouvé table (masculine) in a salmon-pink space (feminine).

GOLDEN RULE

Soften and feminize a "masculine" space with rounded forms, drapes, a rug, fitted carpet, and loose sofa covers—textiles, textiles, and more textiles. To "man up" a feminine room, strip out non-essentials, and choose square, angular furniture arranged in structured groups (two sofas face-to-face, or a sofa opposite two armchairs side-by-side).

hers . . .

Pastel colors and
fifty shades of pink.

Floral motifs, houndstooth
checks, polka dots.

Textiles of all kinds, but
especially velvet, silk, fine
cotton, and fitted carpets.

Rounded, organic,
or circular forms.

. . . and his

Black and white combinations.

Brown, black, gray,
navy blue; bright shades
of blue, red, and yellow;
neutral shades of greige, beige,
and taupe.

Chunky cotton weaves,
wool, and leather.

Geometric motifs
and straight lines: tartan,
chevrons, checks.

Hard surfaces: metal,
wood, glass, and marble,
but *not* ceramics.

Structured forms: cubes
and squares, rectangles,
and angular edges.

for the perfect mix

Avoid a strict 50/50 combination of male/female elements. The result will be oh-so-average. For visually harmonious results, make sure one gender predominates!

Combine masculine materials with feminine shapes, or vice versa: for example, add floral scatter cushions to a chevron-patterned sofa.

At Le Germain restaurant in Paris:
Geometric carpet motifs (masculine)
+ angular, yellow *Sophie* sculpture (masculine)
+ red bookshelves (masculine)
+ round-edged wooden table ("feminized masculine")
+ round ottoman covered in houndstooth check (feminine)

= 80% masculine.

In the bedrooms at the Hôtel Thoumieux in Paris:
Floral wallpaper (I've always loved this—*so* feminine)
+ hand-woven cotton curtains from India (feminine)
+ 1970s-style geometric carpet (masculine)

= 70% feminine.

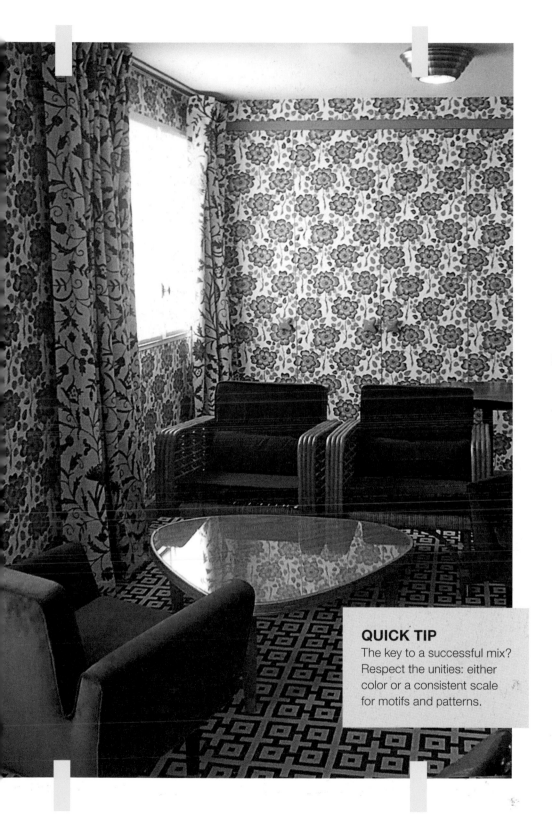

QUICK TIP

The key to a successful mix? Respect the unities: either color or a consistent scale for motifs and patterns.

QUICK TIP

If you're worried about sparking a style riot, calm things down with a strong, plain color: an armchair covered in plain cotton velvet, for example. Or stick to a unifying color scheme—the best way to avoid any glaring *faux pas*.

In this bathroom:
Polka-dot wallpaper (feminine)
+ contemporary Moroccan
zellige tile (masculine)
+ floral curtains (feminine)
+ Italian marble (masculine)
+ curvaceous, pistachio-green
washbasins (feminine)

= 70% feminine.

Incorporate a dash of black-and-white

"seasoning" for a strong, graphic statement in any room. Monochrome features attract the eye and add dynamism.

QUICK TIP
Before investing in wallpaper and fabrics, test them out with large samples in situ (24 × 24 in./60 × 60 cm). Make sure your samples include the complete motif/pattern, to get a clear idea of whether or not your mix will "take." And always ask yourself if you'll be happy to live with it in three years' time.

cheap and cheerful vs. luxury chic

Finding the perfect 30-dollar flea-market lamp for your Perriand table, or a cheap desk that's a dead ringer for the same model by a top designer name, is the decorative equivalent of finding a pair of H&M dress pants to match your YSL tuxedo! Inspired by a commission for *Elle* magazine, I teamed up with IKEA to find the best ways to mix budget chic with designer style.

Choose organic forms—far
more original and eye-catching than
straightforward shapes (such as, say,
a plain square table), and the best way
to avoid an utterly bland, "personality-free"
look. Visually speaking, shape is more
important than quality.

Go for industrial materials (metal, resin, Formica) rather than drab, dark-stained wood—the "tired old standard" of the decoration world.

Fresh, bright colors

(yellow-ocher, pistachio green, blue, orange) are a risk-free option for sofas and seating, while neutral tones (white, off-white) work best for tables and shelving. Like shape, color is visually more important than quality when it comes to furniture and objects.

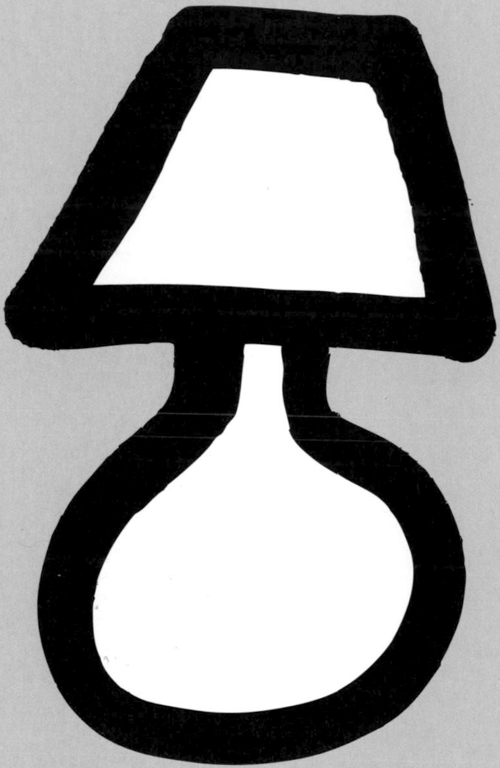

05 successful accessories

Occasional tables, rugs, curtains, lamps.... Accessories
can make or break a room, and choosing them
can be a challenge. But with a touch of imagination,
and two or three basic rules, you're sure to accessorize
with panache.

coffee tables

Personally, I don't like large, monotonous surfaces in the center of my living room. Just as a well-chosen bag can make or break an outfit, so the perfect coffee table can set the tone and provide a visual focus.

Here's how to get it right:

01 The antidote to a large, flat surface: my Bluff table (one of my personal best sellers), conceived as a collection of small tables, with a graphic "checkerboard" effect and sensuous materials.

02 Try coupling (always a good idea): place two tables side-by-side. They can be completely different, or share a family resemblance. Liven them both up with arrangements of small, attractive objects.

03 Three-in-one: a big, leather ottoman serves as a coffee table—add a large, stylish tray—a footrest, and additional seating!

04 Coffee tables invariably make a strong statement. Never be afraid to choose striking shapes or colors, or stylish designer pieces.

05 Not sure you've made the best choice? Keep looking for your dream table, and in the meantime cover up your current one with a designer tray, or a pile of art books topped with a beautiful, treasured object.

no!

. . . to concealing an ugly coffee table under a "hippy" textile. The student dorm look is *out*.

01

02

03

04

curtains and shades

Dress your windows with care: well-chosen drapes or shades will frame (or mask) your outlook, filter the light, and create an atmosphere. Curtains are essential in the bedroom, but dispensable in your living room, unless you find yourself living with unsightly, yellowing window frames or a view of your neighbor's trash cans.

01 A curtain wall: a generous drape running from one wall to the other is the ideal way to hide a radiator, balance a badly proportioned or off-center window, or simplify and structure a room.

02 Shades are great if (1) your window is perfectly proportioned, and (2) there is no space for a curtain rod between the top of your window and the ceiling. In this case, attach the shade directly to your window frame(s).

03 Shower curtains are inherently ugly. Disguise the acres of plastic with a second, outer textile curtain.

QUICK TIP
To make sure you choose the right color for your drapes, hang a fabric sample (preferably a square yard or a square meter) vertically in front of the window—never turn the pattern horizontally (for print fabrics) as this will "skew" the tonal values. Choose a pattern or color two tones lighter than your desired effect, to take account of the light from the window, which invariably makes nearby colors look darker.

04 Choose your curtain color to match the tonal value of your walls, even if you're using a patterned fabric. For white walls, use pastel, beige, or a pale gray-on-white print. For bold colors, apply the "complementary" principle (and respect the tonal values): e.g., mustard-yellow or grass-green curtains for a turquoise room. ● ● ●

08

QUICK TIP
A simple equation gives the ideal "mass" for your curtains: the total fabric width should be one-and-a-half times the length of your curtain rod. Anything beyond that is just too fussy.

05 The "drape" of a curtain is like the cut of a good jacket—there's no room for approximation. For faultless results, I recommend Souveraine Linens from Belgium; or heavy, stonewashed cottons from Jules et Jim and Alter Ego velvet from Élitis, both from Paris (see pp. 174 and 176).

06 Full-length curtains should *just* touch the floor; no more, no less. Don't stint on the depth of your hem: it should be proportionate to the length of the curtain. A minimum of 8 inches (20 cm) is ideal for a curtain 3 yards (2.8 m) long.

07 Combine your curtains with very fine, ecru linen "nets" (I recommend Alabama White no. 5 by Nya Nordiska, www.nya. com), or cotton muslin (optical white from Edmond Petit in Paris). I also love slatted shades, for a summery feel. You can combine slatted shades with full-length "nets," too.

08 Choosing a curtain rod. Keep it ultra-simple, in resin-coated or anthracite-gray metal, extending at least 15 inches (40 cm) either side of the window. I get mine from my home furnishings supplier Home Sails (www.homesails.fr); their range is full of clever ideas and innovative finishes.

no!

- to "A Night at the Opera"-style curtains;
- to curtain rods in rustic wood, polished brass, or stainless steel;
- to frills and ruffles, curtain pelmets, tiebacks, curtains that break over the floor like tumbling waves (unless you live in an eighteenth-century mansion);
- to moiré nylon nets, even if everything comes back in style eventually.

lamps

There are two simple rules for lamps: use a variety of types in each room (floor lamps, table lamps, hanging lamps), and distribute them throughout the space, to surround yourself with light. Seven light sources are ideal for a room measuring around 320 square feet (30 m²), five for a room measuring around 215 square feet (20 m²)—always use an odd number of lights. All you need to do next is choose your lamps, and the right lampshades to go with them!

01 A large floor lamp like my Big Swing, or the Arcolamp from Castiglioni, is an ideal alternative to a ceiling lamp, if your ceiling isn't wired.

02 Never use two wall lamps to "frame" a picture! Install wall lamps side-by-side, in pairs, for a really stylish effect. Think of them as wall sculptures in their own right. I prefer not to position them too high: 5½ feet (1.65 m) from the floor is fine.

yes!
...to dimmer switches. Essential for ceiling lights.

QUICK TIP
Take your lamp base with you when you go shopping for lampshades, and try them out. The best way to find the perfect shape!

03 Like occasional tables, lamps are instant style pointers: don't be afraid to choose bold, unusual designs. •••

04 I buy lots of lamp bases in bric-a-brac shops and flea markets. I love mixing styles from the 1950s, '60s, and '70s.

05 Two unusual lamps placed side-by-side create an original, sculptural statement.

06 Choose colored shades instead of standard white. Beige and rose-pink create a soft, powdery light that is flattering to the skin tone, too. Opt for fabric shades rather than paper. 1970s-style black card shades, lined with gold, are another ultra-chic alternative.

yes!

... to off-center ceiling lights, hanging in a corner, for example. Always a better option than an oppressive, central light source.

no!

... to lampshades dangling from the ceiling. Glo-Ball shades (by Jasper Morrison for Flos) are a great alternative, and my current favorites.

rugs

A rug softens the floor surface, defines a space, muffles sound, and makes a room softer underfoot. In short, it's a vital piece of furniture in its own right—difficult, and a shame, to do without!

01
I love rugs that contribute a strong, graphic note—like striped or zebra-skin motifs. I like placing one over the other, for a striking play of patterns.

02
Soft rugs are essential in the bedroom: shag-pile rugs are great, or look for a Berber rug on your next trip to Morocco.

03
Think big: try one huge rug covering the entire room, leaving a maximum of 8 inches (20 cm) all round, and "embracing" every item of furniture—the last word in chic. I love Fédora's huge woven rugs from Nepal (www.fedoradesign.com), or the fabulous selection at The Rug Company (www.therugcompany.com).

no!
. . . to cow-hide throws or rugs. Zebra-skin is better.

04
A patchwork of Persian carpets or kilims looks great, especially in the living room, but beware of artificially dyed versions—their colors will clash, not blend. Stick to a unifying palette of colors for a harmonious effect.

05
A circular rug is a soothing presence, and always works well in a small space.

yes!
. . . to kitchen rugs: the best way to hide ugly floor tiles. Use a well-worn kilim (these can be machine-washed on your wool cycle), or outdoor rugs from the Manufacture Cogolin in Paris, which can be cleaned with a damp floor-cloth.

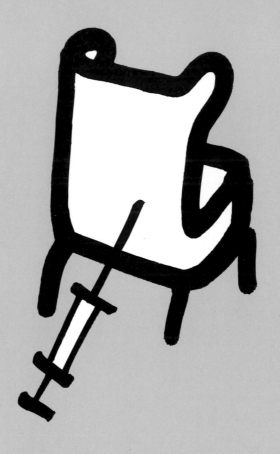

06 quick fixes

Fancy a change of scenery? There's no need to change your address: as with your wardrobe, your interior benefits from a thorough clearing out every now and again. Get into the habit of refreshing key accessories like scatter cushions, throws, and "statement" objects, or customizing furniture items that are showing signs of wear—the best way to keep your home sweet and up to date.

sell it, move it, replace it

Less is more: with this in mind, clear out, give away, or sell those over-familiar items that have followed you from home to home—things you're tired of seeing, things you keep because they came from Granny's or Great-Auntie Agnes's house. Which do you value more: their sentimental value or their visual appeal? Taking the plunge can be difficult, but try it once, at least. You'll soon see how much better you feel after getting rid of a cumbersome item of furniture.

Play musical chairs, or objects, or pictures. Reorganizing your space (while keeping to the rules outlined in section 01) will make it feel like new all over again. If you're low on inspiration, invite friends and neighbors over to brainstorm ideas: fresh pairs of eyes are always helpful.

Keep only the things you really love, however outmoded they may look, and/or quality pieces, which are sure to come back into fashion in years to come. You can always sell them at a good price if you fall out of love with them in the meantime.

Give "borderline" furniture a second chance. Unsure whether to keep it or not? Move it to another room: try your living-room armchair in the hall, or your desk lamp in the kitchen. Seeing things in a new light may save them from the dumpster (or eBay)!

Surround the changes with regular new additions to your "interior wardrobe." Try some striking cushions, a bold vase, a new side table, a colorful stool, an amusing lamp, a round mirror, a framed photograph, or a work of art—anything with genuine "visual presence."

reincarnation

Re-cover your seating,
but think carefully first: a skilled upholsterer will cost more than a new piece of furniture, so is it really worth the expense? For standard IKEA sofas and armchairs, bemz.com sells new loose covers in a great range of fabrics and colors. For "permanent" upholstery, call in the professionals on smaller jobs, like chairs, small armchairs, and stools.

The right stuff: Three
options apply when choosing a new fabric:

1. Velvet: a classic choice that always works well (available from most fabric companies, such as Élitis, Canovas, etc.). Opt for fuschia pink instead of red (to avoid that "Paris brasserie" look), and gray rather than black, to enhance your furniture's lines and silhouettes, and to avoid a dark mass in the middle of your living room (unless you liven it up with pale piping). Other good colors are grass green, mustard, saffron yellow, and brick-orange, which goes with almost anything.

2. Bold, graphic motifs (such as stripes or dots)—you're sure to find something you like at your local fabric supplier. My stamping ground is the rue du Mail, in Paris.

3. Suzani textiles or batik/tie-dye cottons. Now is your chance to put to good use all those souvenirs from your exotic travels.

Look for small but telling details: fringed braid (from Houlès) for your velvet armchair, for example. I used this in some of the bedrooms at Claridge's, and the Coburg Bar at the Connaught, in London—both havens of cozy British chic.

Lampshades are the perfect canvas for your artistic imagination,

especially if they're slightly faded, or bland and uninteresting. At home, I added splashes of color to this tired old shade, but you could try a drawing, or writing a line of poetry in black ink—or let your children do the job! The result may not be high art, but it will always be more original than it was before.

Faded rugs, or mock-Persian replicas inherited

from Auntie can be dyed black or bleached (use a professional carpet-dyer—no point in ruining your washing machine). The results are unexpectedly stylish: you'll keep them for years to come.

Take inspiration from Arman or Maarten Baas: create your own burned

wood Smoke chair! This is obviously not for ulpholstered pieces—use solid wood *only* and only chairs otherwise destined for the dumpster. With care, you might even create your very own work of art.

A win-win option: a fun-fur throw on your old sofa or armchair will extend its life and brighten the rest of the room, too.

07 hip to be square

Everyone knows pink is passé, closets and potted plants are for Grandma, and kitsch is, well, *kitsch*, don't they? Think again! They all rank high on my personal style checklist, so take my advice, and give them a try.

go green

Tall, lush, and luxuriant, today's potted plants are practically trees. Place them either side of your window, like living curtains. *Ficus elastica* or *Philodendron monstera deliciosa* are ideal (just ask your florist). Mine come from Moulié Fleurs in Paris, Truffaut (France's favorite garden store), or Rungis wholesale market. Remember, a balding *ficus* in a Provençal pot placed in a dark corner is *not* what you're after.

la vie en rose

Think pink—remember Schiaparelli?

The latest shades ooze girl-power, warmth, and comfort.

Choose fuschia pink for sofas, armchairs, and ottomans;

sugar pink for beachside settings like my interiors at

the Townhouse hotel; flesh- and salmon-pink for walls

(use a matt finish, or a thin, gloss glaze—coming soon

to my dining room); and, of course, dusty-rose pink, to be

used wherever and whenever you can.

out of the closet

The old-school armoire is today's hippest come-back item, in fabulous contemporary materials like canework, metal, or transparent glass paneling: the antidote to Chinese lacquered cabinets and giant, fur-lined portals to Narnia. Make sure you position your wardrobe to best effect—they're designed to make a bold statement *head-on.*

so kitsch!

Style means having the courage to take risks.

An overly-perfect home isn't a home at all, it's simply a showroom. Everyone should make room for that painting, piece of furniture, decorative object, table service, or multicolored crochet throw that you love no matter what. Beauty is in the eye of the beholder: if you love it, it's your choice, and all the more interesting for *that*.

08 my city guide

A list of my favorite addresses in Paris
and around the world. Add yours!

beirut

Nada Debs

Karen Chekerdjian

Nada Debs

Designer Nada Debs revisits Lebanon's wonderful decorative heritage, bringing it right into the twenty-first century. There's a minimalist touch, too—the legacy of years in Japan—like her best-selling Pebble table, which is my favorite.

Moukhalsieh Street, Building E-1064, Saifi Village, Beirut
Tel. + 961 (0) 1 999 002
www.nadadebs.com

Karen Chekerdjian

Karen Chekerdjian is a rising Lebanese designer, and the creator of the iconic Yo-yo stool, which is fast becoming her signature piece (like my own Bishop stool!).

Derviche Haddad Street, Fayad Building, Port District, Beirut
Tel. + 961 (0) 1 570 572
www.karenchekerdjian.com

Bokja

Karim Bekdache

The grandson of a Lebanese associate
of Jean Royère, Karim Bekdache
grew up in the world of design, and
now runs his own architecture firm
together with a vast gallery presenting
his favorite furniture from the
'50s to the '70s, by top names and
"unknowns."
Kassab Building, Madrid Street,
Mar Mikhael, Beirut
Tel. + 961 (0) 1 566 323
www.karimbekdache.com

Bokja

Hoda Baroudi and Maria Hibri have
been covering vintage furniture with
stunning suzani fabrics, old carpets,
tweed, and velvet for the past twelve
years. Their highly original pieces sell
like wildfire in Milan, New York, and
Paris.
Mukhallassiya Street, Building 332,
Saifi Village, Beirut
Tel. + 961 (0) 1 975 576
www.bokjadesign.com

Smog Gallery

Architect Gregory Gatserelia
specializes in launching the careers of
young creative artists at the frontier
of the design and art worlds and
manufacturing pieces by them.
With highly interesting results.
Dagher Building, 77, Senegal Street,
Karantina, Beirut
Tel. + 961 (0) 1 572 202
www.smogallery.com

Beirut Art Center

In 2010, gallerist Sandra Dagher and
video artist Lamia Joreige transformed
an old furniture factory into an
art center with an international
reputation. Slightly off the beaten
track, but well worth a detour for their
ground-breaking exhibitions.
Jisr El Wati, Corniche an Nahr,
Building 13, Street 97, Zone 66,
Adlieh, Beirut
Tel. + 961 (0) 1 397 018
www.beirutartcenter.org

Agial

.PSLAB

Agial Art Gallery

Saleh Barakat is a passionate, infectiously enthusiastic gallerist, supporting some of the Middle East's most radical, talented artists—including Palestinian-born Abdulrahman Katanani, Ayman Baalbaki (whose work has already featured at Tate London and the Venice Biennale), and Saloua Raouda Choucair, creator of sensational sculptures.

63 Abdul Aziz Street, Hamra District, Beirut
Tel. + 961 (0) 1 345 213
www.agialart.com

Orient 499

Cotton bedlinen made in the Lebanon, soaps using local olive oil, Oriental carpets—every time I set foot in this boutique, I want to buy the whole place!

499 Omar Daouk Street, Hammoud Building, Mina el Hosn, Beirut
Tel. + 961 (0) 1 369 499
www.orient499.com

.PSLAB

I often collaborate with these bespoke lighting solution designers. They are the people behind the lamps at the Monte-Carlo Beach hotel, the Thoumieux, and the Hôtel du Cloître! Their showroom is like a vast laboratory of light.

Nicholas El Turck Street, Mar Michael, Beirut
Tel. + 961 (0) 1 442 546
www.pslab.net

Mömo at the souks

Basta Flea Market

Lebanese and French gallerists have been sourcing choice items in this antiques quarter for years. Some of the merchandise looks a little tired these days, but you can still find old 1950s bamboo armchairs, Bertoïa chairs, vintage chandeliers, and 1950s ceramics (plus plenty of fakes, alas). Worth a visit for the exotic "Oriental flea market" atmosphere.

Kharsa Street, Basta, Beirut

Tawlet

This is the place for daily helpings of regional Lebanese cuisine prepared by country cooks down from the mountains, orchestrated by charismatic owner Kamal Mouzawak. The concept is incredibly popular, and Tawlet is frequently packed with diners from across the city.

Sector 79, Naher Street 12 (Jisr el hadid), Chalhoub Building 22, Beirut
Tel. + 961 (0) 1 448 129
www.tawlet.com

Mömo at the Souks

After Sketch, Mömo, the 404, Andy Wahloo, and the Derrière, Mourad Mazouz, alias Mömo, has opened a new bar-restaurant with a huge terrace in the heart of the new Beirut souks. As always, the venue offers a hip mix of styles, and guaranteed fun.

Jewelry Souk, no. 7, Beirut
Tel. + 961 (0) 1 999 767
www.momo-at-the-souk.com

Hotel Albergo

A charming hotel in a typical 1930s Beirut building, with a terrace to die for.

137, rue Abdel Wahab, El Inglizi, Beirut
Tel. + 961 (0) 1 339 797
www.albergobeirut.com

bombay (mumbai)

Chemould Gallery

Phillips

I adore visiting Bombay antique dealer Farooq Issa, for his colorful chromolithographs by the painter Raja Ravi Varna (1848–1906), antique textiles embroidered with scenes from Indian mythology, glass paintings from the early twentieth century, and a host of other objects, furniture, and artwork, always of impeccable quality.
Madam Cama Road, opposite the Regal Cinema, Mumbai 400001
Tel. + 91 22 2202 0564
www.phillipsantiques.com

Bungalow 8

Bombay's essential address for all things art deco. Three floors in a superb, listed block provide the perfect showcase for a thousand-and-one finds courtesy of antique dealer Maithili Ahluwalia, from vintage furniture to Indian artisan textiles and objects with a contemporary twist—perfect for export!
Grants Building, 1st, 2nd, and 3rd floors, 17 Arthur Bunder Road, Colaba, Mumbai 400005
Tel. + 91 22 2281 9880
www.bungaloweight.com

Chemould Prescott Road Gallery

Chemould Gallery's stable includes the cream of Indian contemporary art: Atul Dodiya and Gigi Scavia (who represented his country recently at the Venice Biennale). Chemould also attends art fairs around the world, if you can't come to Bombay!
Prescott Road, Queens Mansion (3rd floor), G. Talwatkar Marg, Fort, Mumbai 400001
Tel. + 91 22 2200 0211
www.gallerychemould.com

Dr. Bhau Daji Lad Museum

Chor Baazar

Dr. Bhau Daji Lad Museum

Bombay's former Victoria & Albert Museum is a real gem, and quite unexpected: a ravishing Palladian villa with pistachio-green walls and gilded pillar capitals, fresh from a recent, five year restoration program. The collection features nineteenth-century work from the Indian Arts & Crafts movement.

91/A, Rani Baug, Dr. Ambedkar Marg, Byculla East, Mumbai, Maharashtra 400027
Tel. + 91 22 2373 1234
www.bdlmuseum.org

Chor Bazaar

I never visit a city without dropping in on its flea market. This one is a real Aladdin's Cave, with an eclectic array of treasures from crystal chandeliers to vintage mirrors, colored glass lanterns, and a scattering of vintage furniture, in a uniquely Indian atmosphere.

Mutton Street, Mumbai

Hamilton Studio

At 82 years of age, Ranjit Madhavji—photographer to India's top British dignitaries, maharajahs, and the Bollywood stars of the 1960s—is still busy as a society snapper, capturing the local gentry and their marriageable offspring. His studio hasn't changed one iota in decades and is a historic monument in its own right, a must-see before it disappears forever.

NTC House, Narotam Moraji Marg, Ballard Estate, Mumbai 400038
Tel. + 91 22 2261 4544

istanbul

Abdulla

A la Turca Kilim House

A la Turca Kilim House

In a townhouse in Istanbul's Çurkurcuma district, Erkal Aksoy presents four floors of old kilims, antiques, and unusual objects, reflecting their collector's impeccable taste.

**Faik Paşa Caddesi No. 4,
Çukurcuma, Cihangir, Istanbul
Tel. + 90 (0) 212 245 29 33
www.alaturcahouse.com**

Hall Shop

For contemporary Orientalist furniture by designer Christopher Hall.

**Faik Paşa Caddesi, No. 6,
Çukurcuma, Cihangir, Istanbul
Tel. + 90 (0) 212 292 95 90
www.hallistanbul.com**

Abdulla

This boutique in the heart of the grand bazaar is the place for pestemal (traditional hammam towels). Hand-woven and tinted with natural, vegetable dyes, they're perfect for the poolside, too.

**Halicilar Caddesi 58–60
Kapaliçarşi (Grand Bazaar), Istanbul
Tel. + 90 (0) 212 526 30 70
and
Alibaba Türbe Sokak No. 25
Nurosmaniye, 34440 Istanbul
www.abdulla.com**

Yastık by Rifat Özbek

Autoban

Autoban

This unmissable showroom presents
the full range of work by architecture
and design stars Seyhan Özdemir
and Sefer Çaglar—in particular,
their wonderful wooden lamps. My
favorites are the Big Lamp, the
Magnolia Lamp, and the Wing Lamp.
**Sinanpaşa Mah, Süleyman Seba
Cad. No. 16–20, Akaretler Beşiktaş,
34357 Istanbul
Tel. + 90 (0) 212 236 92 46
www.autoban212.com**

Yastik by Rifat Özbek

This dazzling concept boutique,
opened by celebrated Turkish stylist
Rifat Özbek, sells his fashion
creations and brightly colored, exotic
scatter cushion designs, ranged on
shelves like tomes in a bookshop.
People snap them up like "souvenir
postcards" of Istanbul!
**Şakayik Sokak, Olcay Apt. No. 13/1
Teşvikiye, Şişli, Istanbul
Tel. + 90 (0) 212 240 87 31
www.yastikbyrifatozbek.com**

cape town

The African Market

Tribal Trends

The V&A Waterfront

An essential stop on Cape Town's art and design trail, for the giant Coca Cola-crate sculpture (Elliot the Cratefan) by leading South African artist Porky Hefer, who is equally well known for his wonderful, poetic "nest" sculptures.

Long Street

Cape Town's top shopping street is crammed with boutiques selling local crafts, with a wealth of original finds. Explore at leisure, or get straight to the point at:

Tribal Trends

The place for chic handicrafts. I love Mustard Seed's flower-shaped bowls, dishes, and plates, and Ardemore's Zulu "animal" tableware: the ultimate "kitsch comeback." It's a little pricey, but each piece is unique. Tribal Trends sells picture frames, cushions, and contemporary/traditional furniture, too, by South African artists and designers.
Winchester House, 72–74 Long Street, Cape Town 8001
Tel. + 27 (0) 21 423 8008

The African Market

A great shop selling a comprehensive range of local handicrafts.
76 Long Street, Cape Town 8001
Tel. + 27 (0) 21 426 4478

What if the World

Woodstock

Cape Town's oldest neighborhood is an unmissable stop, and a highly hip part of town, full of huge art galleries, designer showrooms, restaurants, and fashion boutiques. Woodstock is also home to the Old Biscuit Mill organic market (on weekends).

Essential Woodstock addresses are:

Stevenson

One of the city's best contemporary art galleries. I love Hylton Nel's ceramics, and photographs by Guy Tillim and Pieter Hugo.
Buchanan Building, 160 Sir Lowry Road, Woodstock, Cape Town 7925
Tel. + 27 (0) 21 462 1500
www.stevenson.info

What if the World

An essential port of call to discover South Africa's stable of emerging contemporary artists.
1 Argyle Street, Woodstock, Cape Town 7925
Tel. + 27 (0) 21 802 3111
www.whatiftheworld.com

Gregor Jenkin Studio

I love their delicate, stylish furniture.
1 Argyle Street, Woodstock, Cape Town 7925
Tel. + 27 (0) 21 424 1840
www.gregorjenkin.com

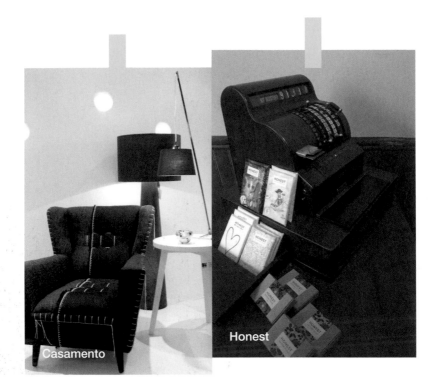

Casamento

Honest

Goodman Gallery

Somewhat off the beaten track, but don't be discouraged: the exhibitions here make it all worthwhile. This is one of South Africa's flagship galleries, and a leading light on the international contemporary scene, too. A regular face at Art Basel and FIAC, in Paris, Goodman represents a stable of politically committed artists including Ghada Amer, Kader Attia, Kendel Geers, and Sigalit Landau.
3rd floor, Fairweather House,
176 Sir Lowry Road, Woodstock,
Cape Town 7925
Tel. + 27 (0) 21 462 7573

Casamento

An artisan upholsterer specializing in patchwork and plain seating, with an understated style and inspirational, charming results.
160 Albert Road, Woodstock,
Cape Town 7925
Tel. + 27 (0) 21 448 6183
www.casamento.co.za

Honest

A small chocolate shop frequented by the whole of Cape Town, transformed by the owners into one of the city's most charming venues, with delicate, homemade, organic chocolate goodies to match!
66 Wale Street, Cape Town 8001
Tel. + 27 (0) 21 423 8762
www.honestchocolate.co.za

Test Kitchen

Mount Nelson Hotel

Test Kitchen

Gourmets, be warned! This restaurant in the Old Biscuit Mill is Cape Town's answer to Copenhagen's Noma (voted the Best Restaurant in the World). Chef Luc Dale-Robert is a leading light in contemporary cuisine.

The Old Biscuit Mill, 375 Albert Road, Woodstock, Cape Town 7925 Tel. + 27 (0) 21 447 2337 www.thetestkitchen.co.za

Mount Nelson Hotel

This "Old Colonial" hotel, with its charming garden, is one of the city's nicest places to stay. I always feel like moving in and staying for a few weeks, if not months! It's perfect for shopping, too, being just a stone's throw from Long Street.

76 Orange Street, Cape Town 8001 Tel. + 27 (0) 21 483 1000 www.mountnelson.co.za

lisbon

Palacio de Fronteira

1300 Taberna, LX Factory

The LX Factory, an old industrial site beside the Tagus river, has become one of Lisbon's hippest places, with an array of bars and fashion boutiques. The newest arrival is this restaurant, decorated with old chandeliers, patchwork sofas, huge clocks, and family portraits —all of which are for sale!

Rua Rodrigues Faria 103, 1300 Lisbon

Tel. + 351 213 649 170

www.1300taberna.com

A Vida Portuguesa

Ex-journalist Catherine Portas produces ineffably charming, contemporary updates of typical, old-fashioned Portuguese creations. I love her woven Alentejo bedcovers, and Emilio Braga's beautiful notebooks.

Rua Anchieta 11, 1200-023 Chiado, Lisbon

Tel. + 351 213 465 073

www.avidaportuguesa.com

Caza das Vellas Loreto

This Lisbon institution has produced altar and household candles for over two hundred years. The place is well worth a visit, especially for its white candles delicately carved with lacy motifs. Unchanged since it first opened, the setting is like a miniature church crypt. Absolutely unique.

Rua Loreto 53–55, 1200-241 Lisbon

Tel. + 351 213 425 387

www.cazavellasloreto.com

Mude

Hotel Ritz

Palacio de Fronteira

The most magical building in Lisbon is this seventeenth-century palace, with its Italian gardens, its azulejos tiled pavilion, and its elegant black swans. It's still occupied by a descendant of one of Portugal's grandest families, hence visiting hours are restricted: be sure to call ahead or check online if you don't want to find the gates firmly closed.

Largo de São Domingos de Benfica 1, 1500-554 Lisbon
Tel. + 351 217 782 023
www.fronteira-alorna.pt

Mude

130,000 square feet (12,000 m²) devoted to fashion and design, in a remodeled bank building reminiscent of Paris's Palais de Tokyo. Fabulous!

Rua Augusta 24, 1100-053 Lisbon
Tel. + 351 218 886 117
www.mude.pt

Museu Berardo

José Berardo is not only one of Portugal's wealthiest entrepreneurs, he's also one of Europe's best-known art collectors, with works by Picasso, Miró, Dalí, Bacon, and Warhol, among others. This collection is a rich panorama of modern and contemporary art.

Praço do Imperio, 1449-003 Lisbon
Tel. + 351 213 612 878
www.museuberardo.com

Four Seasons Hotel Ritz Lisbon

I adore this 1950s-style retro-glam palace hotel by Henri Samuel. If you can't afford a room, you can always sip a drink at the bar, rubbing elbows with the Lisboan elite.

Rua Rodrigo da Fonseca 88, 1099-039 Lisbon
Tel. + 351 213 811 400
www.fourseasons.com/lisbon

london

Liberty

The finest selection of items you'll find in almost any department store! Every time I visit, I discover sensational new wallpaper manufacturers and textile designers, like Neisha Grosland. I love the way they "stage" their furniture and objects (on the 4th floor), like a slightly chaotic but hugely charming antique dealer's emporium.

Regent Street, London W1B 5AH
Tel. + 44 (0) 20 7734 1234
www.liberty.co.uk

Established and Sons

Opened by *Wallpaper* magazine cofounder Alasdhair Willis, among others, this gallery produces designer furniture from a faultless list of names including Richard Woods. Well worth a visit.

5–7 Wenlock Road, London N1 7SL
Tel. + 44 (0) 20 7608 0990
www.establishedandsons.com

Established and Sons

Gallery Fumi

Gallery Fumi

This youthful design gallery specializes in emerging names like the highly talented Jeremy Wintrebert: I adore his blown-glass pieces.

16 Hoxton Square, London N1 6NT
Tel. + 44 (0) 20 7490 2366
www.galleryfumi.com

Cath Kidston

I love her retro, flowery PVC cotton cloths: English kitsch at its very best!
322 King's Road, London SW3 4RP
Tel. + 44 (0) 20 7351 7335
www.cathkidston.co.uk

Dover Street Market

An astonishing place in the heart of ultra-chic Mayfair, with a state-of-the-art fashion section, and windows by leading artists and designers.
17–18 Dover Street, London W1S 4LT
Tel. + 44 (0) 20 7518 0680
www.doverstreetmarket.com

Claridge's

The Connaught

Tom Dixon

Tom Dixon's wonderful world of stuff is all on show in the Wharf Building at Portobello Dock. The flagship store of the English designer also shows work by friends, including Piet Hein Eek. Stay for lunch at his Dock Kitchen restaurant, serving delicious organic food by chef Stevie Parle.

**Wharf Building, Portobello Dock,
344 Ladbroke Grove,
London W10 5BU
Tel. + 44 (0) 20 7400 0500 and
+ 44 (0) 20 7183 8544 (online shop)
www.tomdixon.net**

Sketch

The years go by, but this address is a permanent—if ever-changing—fixture. Mömo has just given artist Martin Creed carte blanche to transform the dining room—with a glorious mix-and-match look, from the chairs to the forks. And it works!

**9 Conduit Street, London W1S 2XG
Tel. + 44 (0) 20 7659 4500
www.sketch.uk.com**

Claridge's

London's chicest hotel, and the place for afternoon tea. If you're staying the night, be sure to ask for one of my decorated suites!

**49 Brook Street, London W1K 4HR
Tel. + 44 (0) 20 7629 8860
www.claridges.co.uk**

The Connaught

This London institution is located in a beautiful Edwardian townhouse. Try a drink at the Coburg Bar, or dine in style at Hélène Darroze's fabulous restaurant.

**16 Carlos Place, London W1K 2AL
Tel + 44 (0) 20 7499 7070
www.the-connaught.co.uk**

mexico city

Chic By Accident

ADN

ADN

In Mexico City's chic Polanco neighborhood, ADN presents a selection of twentieth-century "antiques" and new work by young Mexican designers, offering a fresh take on traditional furniture. (The store's name means DNA in Spanish.)

Av. Moliere 62, Col. Polanco, Mexico City
Tel. + 52 55 5511 5521
www.adngaleria.mx

Chic By Accident

Frenchman Emmanuel Picault deals in contemporary "antiques," displayed in theatrical fashion and with considerable flair, over several floors of a 1920s townhouse in the city's Roma district. Furniture, lighting, and unusual objects combine to create a signature style, subsequently reflected in Picault's decor for Mexico City's current hippest nightclub, the M.N. Roy, noted for its "futurist Aztec" look. Two places not to be missed.

Alvaro Obregon 49, Col. Roma Norte, Mexico City
Tel. + 52 55 5511 1312
www.chicbyaccident.com

Kurimanzutto Gallery

Pirwi

Pirwi

The showroom for new work by
contemporary designers.
Alejandro Dumas 124, Col. Polanco,
11560 Mexico City
Tel. + 52 55 1579 6514
www.pirwi.com

Kurimanzutto Gallery

The city's flagship gallery represents
Mexico's finest contemporary artists,
incuding Gabriel Orozco, Carlos
Amorales, and Damian Ortega.
Gobernador Rafael Rebollar 94,
San Miguel Chapultepec, Miguel
Hidalgo, 11850 Mexico City
Tel. + 52 55 5256 2408
www.kurimanzutto.com

San Angel market

Try to combine a visit to Diego
Rivera's studio with a trip to the
Saturday market in San Angel. This
is where I found the woven wool
blankets, embroidered tablecloths,
and pine-needle baskets for the city's
Condesa df hotel (illustrated on p. 57).
The best source in town for authentic
Mexican craftwork.

Museo Anahuacalli

Condesa df

Casa Luis Barragán

One of my favorite addresses in Mexico City. I remember getting goose bumps the first time I visited the house of this grand master of Mexican architecture. His home remains furnished just as he left it, with his belongings, records, and books still scattered around: you feel he might walk back in at any moment.

General Francisco Ramírez 12–14, Col. Ampliación Daniel Garza, 11840 Mexico City
Tel. + 52 55 5515 4908
www.casaluisbarragan.org

Museo Diego Rivera Anahuacalli

This extraordinary building, reminiscent of an Aztec pyramid, was designed by the painter Diego Rivera to house his huge collection of pre-Columbian art. A truly remarkable place.

Museo 150, San Pablo Tepetlapa, Coyoacán, 04620 Mexico City
Tel. + 52 55 5617 4310
www.museoanahuacalli.org.mx

Condesa df

Located in the eponymous Condesa district, this was one of the very first hotels I designed, in 2003. Enjoy a drink on the terrace, which has lovely views of the magnificent gardens. Be sure to visit the Downtown, one of the latest hotels opened by the Habita group, located in a sixteenth-century palace in Mexico City's historic center. It combines all my favorite things: a magnificent historic building, and an interior reworked by two talented young Mexican architects, Javier Serrano and Abraham Cherem. A great success.

Condesa df
Av. Veracruz 102, Col. Condesa, 06700 Mexico City
Tel. + 52 55 5241 2600
www.condesadf.com

Downtown
Isabel la Católica 30, Col. Centro, Mexico City
Tel. + 52 55 5130 6830
www.downtownmexico.com

los angeles

JF Chen

Maxfield's

JF Chen

J.F. Chen has been a passionate collector of modern antiques and bric-a-brac for over forty years, embracing all styles, exhibiting and selling his finds in an enormous warehouse full to the brim with (chiefly) twentieth-century design. He has specialized in this area for the past decade or so, although you may spot the occasional fine Japanese ceramic, or other artworks, too.

941 North Highland Avenue,
Los Angeles, CA 90038
Tel. + 1 310 559 2436
www.jfchen.com

Maxfield's

L.A.'s cult fashion store is hidden away in a concrete bunker in the Melrose district. The place that launched the career of Rick Melrose still offers the best cutting-edge designers, plus a range of vintage clothing, jewelry, and bags. The theatrical "sets" and sculptural installations throughout the store create a unique atmosphere.

8825 Melrose Avenue, Los Angeles, CA 90069
Tel. + 1 310 274 8800
www.maxfieldla.com

Blackman Cruz

Bountiful on Abbot Kinney

Blackman Cruz

A trip to this unusual antiques store is always fun. Owners Adam Blackman and David Cruz have truly unique taste in extraordinary objects of all styles and periods.

836 North Highland Avenue, Los Angeles, CA 90038
Tel. + 1 323 466 8600
www.blackmancruz.com

Bountiful on Abbot Kinney

Hard to resist the display windows of this store, packed from floor to ceiling with pastel-colored glassware in all shades.

1335 Abbot Kinney Boulevard, Los Angeles, CA 90291
Tel. + 1 310 450 3620
www.bountifulhome.com

Matthew Marks Gallery

New York gallerist Matthew Marks has opened a new L.A. showcase presenting his list of top names, including Jasper Johns, Brice Marden, Robert Gober, and Nan Goldin. The other big draw is the facade by Ellsworth Kelly—a work of art in its own right.

1062 North Orange Grove, Los Angeles, CA 90046
Tel. + 1 323 654 1830
www.matthewmarks.com

milan

Nilufar

Nina Yashar combines fabulous vintage pieces by Carlo Mollino, Gaetano Pesce, and Finn Juhl with work by today's leading young designers—such as Fabien Capello or Martino Gamper—in stunning presentations.
Via della Spiqa 32, 20121 Milan, Tel. + 39 02 780193
www.nilufar.com

Rossana Orlandi

The epicenter of Milan's design scene, in a charming brick building that was once a post office. The only place to be during Milan Design Week.
Via Matteo Bandello 14–16, 20123 Milan
Tel. + 39 02 4674471
www.rossanaorlandi.com

Exits

The great Italian designer and architect Michele de Lucchi has opened his first gallery, in a raw space showcasing his own latest creations plus a careful selection of other work, from Established & Son and Moorman.
Via Varese 14, 20121 Milan
Tel. + 39 02 36550249
www.exits.it

La Rinascente

10 Corso Como

La Rinascente

A "design supermarket" offering 17,200 square feet (1,600 m²) of home items from the likes of Alessi, Kartell, Fornasetti, and Pols Potten.

Piazza Duomo, via Santa Radegonda 1, 20121 Milan
Tel. + 39 02 88521
www.rinascente.it

10 Corso Como

Carla Sozzani's concept store has been a Mecca for Milanese fashion, photography, and fine art publishing for the past twenty years. I stop by (almost) every time I'm in town. And when the weather's nice, it's my favorite place for lunch in the garden!

Corso Como 10, 20154 Milan
Tel. + 39 02 29002674
www.10corsocomo.com

G. Lorenzi

This gracious old townhouse offers a crash course in the art of fine living. Here you'll find silver egg-cup sets and mother-of-pearl caviar services, all beautifully crafted, incredibly sophisticated, and extremely hard to find anywhere else. I adore their accessories in natural horn, especially the bathroom collection.

Via Montenapoleone 9, Milan
Tel. + 39 02 76022848
www.lorenzi.it

new york

ABC Carpet & Home

Wyeth

ABC Carpet & Home

This high temple of home decoration
is an essential stop, with seven
floors of furniture, carpets, bedlinen,
textiles, and accessories. The range
of styles is bewildering, from the
ultra-kitsch to the super-chic, like
hand-woven cushions by Judy Ross
(some of which I stock in my Paris
showroom). If you don't want to
browse, save time and make straight
for the "contemporary" floors.
**881 and 888 Broadway, at E 19th
Street, New York, NY 10003
Tel. + 1 212 473 3000
www.abchome.com**

Wyeth

The owners of this vast space travel
the world in search of the finest
vintage Scandinavian and American
furniture, beautifully presented here
in a series of inspiring room-sets.
Their own collection of furniture
reflects the same Modernist spirit.
**315 Spring Street, New York,
NY 10013
Tel. + 1 212 243 3661
www.wyethome.com**

Ralph Pucci

BDDW

Ralph Pucci

Ralph Pucci's two-story loft space
is a mini-museum of designer chic,
featuring top American names like
Vladimir Kagan and Jens Risom, and
emerging stars like David Weeks.
Pucci also has a soft spot for French
designers like Andrée Putman (his
mentor, back in 1986), Patrick Naggar,
Paul Mathieu, and yours truly! He
has an incomparable talent for mixing
elegance and creativity, with often
spectacular sets that change every
three months.

**11th and 12th floors, 44 W 18th
Street, New York, NY 10011
Tel. + 1 212 633 0452
www.ralphpucci.net**

BDDW

Tyler Hays was an artist before
dedicating himself to design, although
his sculptural roots are clear in pieces
such as his stunning walnut-trunk
tables, or the cut logs piled high
against the walls of his studio to
spectacular effect. His work combines
America's great craft tradition with
the essence of Shaker style, revisited
with a contemporary twist and a
feeling for poetic detail.

**5 Crosby Street, New York,
NY 10013
Tel. + 1 212 625 1230
www.bddw.com**

John Derian

John Derian

John Derian's East Village design shrine sells his signature dishes, plates, lamps, and vases, decorated with clever cut-outs and collages of old prints. Be sure to visit his second space next door, where work by his favorite designers is displayed with vintage furniture. Both places ooze style and charm.

6 and 10 E 2nd Street, New York, NY 10003

Tel. + 1 212 677 3917

www.johnderian.com

Chelsea galleries

No visit to New York, however short, is complete without a visit to Chelsea's gallery quarter, between 20th and 26th Streets. My favorites are Gagosian (*who else?*), Zwirner (the other "king of New York"), and Sonnabend. For a change of scene, I head to the top floor of the Americano (the only hotel in the neighborhood) for a drink on the terrace.

518 W 27th Street, New York, NY 10001

Tel. + 1 212 525 0000

www.hotel-americano.com

Gagosian

Larry Gagosian has dedicated his latest Manhattan space to (relatively) reasonably priced limited editions from his stable of artists. Look out for Jeff Koons's *Puppy*, or multicolored chairs by Franz West (my favorites).

980 Madison Avenue, New York, NY 10075

Tel. + 1 212 744 2313

www.gagosian.com

Bookmarc

Pearl Paint

Pearl Paint

Pearl Paint is a supplier of art materials, frequented by New Yorkers of all walks of life, from top contemporary artists to penniless students and amateur "Sunday" painters. The store, on Canal Street in Chinatown, has been open since 1933 (forever, in American terms!) and sells literally everything. I buy huge consignments of fluorescent sticky tape here, for use in my studio.

308 Canal Street, New York, NY 10013

Tel. + 1 212 431 7932

www.pearlpaint.com

Bookmarc

Marc Jacobs has had the very good idea of dotting his small boutiques around the cobbled streets of the West Village. The "chain" includes Bookmarc, a tiny bookshop selling his own, ultra-hip selection of fine art, fashion, photography, and design books. Always fascinating.

400 Bleecker Street, New York, NY 10014

Tel. + 1 212 620 4021

www.marcjacobs.com/bookmarc

Brooklyn Flea Market

Dia:Beacon

Dia:Beacon

If you want to escape New York's madding crowds, try a visit to the Dia Art Foundation in Beacon. Not that New York is exactly short of art—I never tire of the MoMA, the Whitney, the Guggenheim, and Chelsea's galleries—but the Foundation's Beacon location is stunning. The old Nabisco factory on the shores of the Hudson River has been completely transformed to create an immaculate space housing a remarkable collection of minimalist and conceptual work. The vast installations by Walter de Marie and Michael Haizer are my personal favorites: touching and inspiring.

3 Beekman Street, Beacon, NY 12508

Tel. + 1 845 440 0100

www.diabeacon.org

Brooklyn Flea Market, Fort Greene

Brooklyn Flea Market has knocked Chelsea's market off its perch. Even hardened Manhattanites are prepared to cross the bridge these days, to Fort Greene (Spike Lee's beloved bit of Brooklyn), for an eclectic mix of objects, furniture, and curios of all kinds. Don't miss the latest work from young Brooklyn-based designers.

176 Lafayette Avenue, Brooklyn, NY 11238

Every Saturday, 10 a.m. to 5 p.m.

Monkey Bar

Boom Boom Room

Boom Boom Room

Run by socialite André Balasz, New York's most select nightclub—aka Top of the Standard at The Standard hotel—offers a 360-degree view over the city, and a flashback to 1940s decor, Hollywood-style.

848 Washington Street, at W 13th Street, New York, NY 10014
Tel. + 1 212 645 4646
www.standardhotels.com

Monkey Bar

A New York legend and once the city's hottest nightspot, the Monkey has been given a new lease of life thanks to *Vanity Fair* supremo Graydon Carter. Follow in the footsteps of Ernest Hemingway, Frank Sinatra, and Ava Gardner.

60 E 54th Street, New York, NY 10014
Tel. + 1 212 308 2950
www.monkeybarnewyork.com

The Mercer

An unrivaled classic. I always stay at this hotel when I'm in town.

147 Mercer Street, Soho, New York, NY 10012
Tel. + 1 212 966 6060
www.mercerhotel.com

paris

Le Manach

FABRICS AND WALLPAPERS

Jules et Jim

Excellent selection of fabrics and wallpapers from small manufacturers. My personal favorites are the screen-printed collection by Raoul Textiles, graphic patterned papers and fabrics from Neisha Crosland, and Florence Broadhurst's big printed motifs. For plain fabrics, I love the cotton and linen ranges by Souveraine. NB: the showroom isn't at street level; head for the second floor.

1 rue Thérèse, 75001 Paris
Tel. + 33 (0) 1 43 14 02 10
www.julesetjim.fr

Bisson-Bruneel

This family-run business is the place for fine white "nets," with a huge choice of very pretty, plain white cottons.

21 place des Vosges, 75003 Paris
Tel. + 33 (0) 1 40 29 95 81
www.bisson-bruneel.com

Le Manach

This distinguished house, with a two-hundred-year history, is my favorite place for toile de Tours—in fact, they're the only company still making it. I love their Écailles, Croisillon, and Blason designs, which I often use for chair seats and sofas.

31 rue du Quatre-Septembre,
75002 Paris
Tel. + 33 (0) 1 47 42 52 94
www.lemanach.fr

Au fil des couleurs

Au fil des couleurs

An Aladdin's cave of classic and modern wallpapers, selling all the major manufacturers, so you're guaranteed to find what you're after! They even provide swatches to try out at home, but take my tip: don't be afraid to buy one whole roll; this is really the only way to get the full effect and avoid a costly mistake.
31 rue de l'Abbé Grégoire, 75006 Paris
Tel. + 33 (0) 1 45 44 74 00
www.aufildescouleurs.com

Rubelli

Dominique Kieffer's Oseille Sauvage linen collection is ideal for full-length curtains that hang perfectly.
11 rue de l'Abbaye, 75006 Paris
Tel. + 33 (0) 1 43 54 27 77
www.rubelli.com

Casal

I'm a fan of Luciano Marcato velvets, on sale here. The collection offers impeccable quality and perfectly judged colors. Their mustard yellow is my current favorite!
40 rue des Saints-Pères, 75007 Paris
Tel. + 33 (0) 1 44 39 07 07
www.casal.fr

Pierre Frey

A historic manufacturer, selling wonderful silk velvets.
2 rue de Fürstenberg, 75006 Paris
Tel. + 33 (0) 1 46 33 73 00
www.pierrefrey.com

Élitis

Dedar

Nya Nordiska

For plain cottons, perfect for curtains.
40 rue des Saint-Pères, 75007 Paris
Tel. + 33 (0) 1 45 48 04 05
www.nya.com

Osborne & Little

Authentic English wallpapers,
beautifully printed.
7 rue de Fürstenberg, 75007 Paris
Tel. + 33 (0) 1 56 81 02 66
www.osborneandlittle.com

Dedar

For their range of wallpapers and
fabrics by Hermès.
20 rue Bonaparte, 75006 Paris
Tel. + 33 (0) 1 56 81 10 98
www.dedar.com

Élitis

I love their Totem range of cotton
velvets, with a rich choice of colors.
35 rue de Bellechasse, 75007 Paris
Tel. + 33 (0) 1 45 51 51 00
www.elitis.fr

Houlès

The boutique for braids and
haberdashery. This is the place for
those fringed and pom-pom trims
that will give your old armchair a
second life.
18 rue Saint-Nicolas, 75012 Paris
Tel. + 33 (0) 1 43 44 65 19
www.houles.com

Houlès

Ido Diffusion

LEATHER

Ido Diffusion

The place to go for leathers to cover your chairs and sofas. J. Robert Scott leathers are the *crème de la crème*, with wonderfully soft skins in colors you won't find anywhere else. Their range of beiges, taupes, and browns is wonderful. I also love Moore and Giles, especially their Notting Hill range. By appointment only.

24 rue Mayet, 75006 Paris
Tel. + 33 (0) 1 47 34 38 61
www.ido-diffusion.com

PAINT AND WALL FABRICS

Atelier Lucien Tourtoulou

It's often so difficult to find the right paint color. Discovering Lucien Tourtoulou has solved the problem for me! An artist in his own right, Lucien presents a vast array of fabrics and paints for floors and walls alike, in a subtle range of colors.

57 bis rue de Tocqueville,
75017 Paris
Tel. + 33 (0) 1 47 54 06 72

Pierre Bonnefille

Bonnefille's Argile paints use natural pigments inspired by earth colors. He offers genuine expertise, especially for his fabulous collection of textured wall treatments.

5 rue Bréguet, 75009 Paris
Tel. + 33 (0)1 43 55 06 84
www.pierrebonnefille.com

La Manufacture Cogolin

Deyrolle

RUGS AND CARPETS

Codimat

Carpets and rugs are made to order, and you can personalize the colors. The Madeleine Castaing range—especially the leopardskin print—is quite wonderful, and is perfect for bedrooms. Look out for the psychedelic motifs in their terrific 1960s collection.

63–65 rue du Cherche-Midi, 75007 Paris

Tel. + 33 (0) 1 45 44 68 20

www.codimatcollection.com

La Manufacture Cogolin

Founded in 1924, this distinguished house still uses traditional looms: the Rolls Royce of textile weaving! I love their plaited straw carpets and woven rugs in jute and wool.

30 rue des Saints-Pères, 75007 Paris

Tel. + 33 (0) 1 40 49 04 30

www.tapis-cogolin.com

Hartley's of Paris

One of the very best places for plain wool fitted carpets, with a fabulous range of colors, plus stair runners in graphic patterns (the Jacquard collection). Hartley's will lay your carpet, too, which is very good news.

87 rue de Monceau, 75008 Paris

Tel. + 33 (0) 1 53 04 06 86

www.hartleys-of-paris.com

Deyrolle

This exotic, fantastical shop is where I buy my zebra skins, and the glass-fronted butterfly cases in which I present my fabric samples and materials, piece by piece.

46 rue du Bac, 75007 Paris

Tel. + 33 (0) 1 42 22 32 21

www.deyrolle.com

CERAMIC AND STONE TILE

Palatino

Paris's biggest selection of floor and wall coverings, including stone, tile, terra-cotta, cement, zellige, and more. Their range is huge, and highly original, presented in pull-out drawers, like a vast library.

10 rue du Moulin-Noir,
92000 Nanterre
Tel. + 33 (0) 1 42 04 90 30
www.palatino.tr

Le 332

This ultra-chic showroom presents work by cabinetmaker SIGébène and automated home environment specialist Henri, and marbles by EDM.

332 rue Saint-Honoré, 75001 Paris
Tel. + 33 (0) 1 55 35 92 54
www.le332.com

DIY, DOOR KNOBS, AND HANDLES

BHV

I love the BHV's second-floor department selling knobs and handles for doors and cupboards. Check out their wonderfully atmospheric DIY basement, too.

52 rue de Rivoli, 75004 Paris
Tel. + 33 (0) 9 77 40 14 00
www.bhv.fr

La Quincaillerie

An excellent selection of knobs and handles for doors and cupboards, plus door-stop mechanisms, latches, and bolts, all clearly visible on helpful display panels. I adore Gio Ponti's Puddler handles, and the collection by John Pawson.

3 and 4 boulevard Saint-Germain,
75005 Paris
Tel. + 33 (0) 1 46 33 66 71 and
(0) 1 55 42 98 01
www.laquincaillerie.com

Bronze de France

This distinguished house sells everything from casement bolts and Directoire knobs to handcrafted Empire, art deco, and contemporary designs. They also stock my Las Cases range of door knobs and handles.

73 avenue Daumesnil, 75012 Paris
Tel. + 33 (0) 1 42 44 24 07
www.bronze-de-France.com

LIGHTING

Flos

This is where I buy my Glo-ball ceiling lamps by Jasper Morrison. They come in a range of sizes and are extremely easy to use, and can be installed as wall lights in bathrooms and kitchens, too: an effective, multipurpose lighting solution.

15 rue de Bourgogne, 75007 Paris
Tel. + 33 (0) 1 53 85 49 93
www.flosfrance.com

Inédit

Pouenat

Inédit

Sébastien Pinault offers excellent advice and a great selection of spotlights (especially the Modulart range), plus lamps and metal switches—I recommend the Meljac range. He will also design lighting solutions tailored to your home. His Nautic range is the perfect solution to the eternal problem of attractive outdoor lighting.

25 rue de Cléry, 75002 Paris
Tel. + 33 (0) 1 47 00 76 76
www.inedit-lighting.com

Pouenat

When Jacques Rayet took over this historic manufacturer of fine metalwork for cabinets and lamps (est. 1880), he had the very good sense to ask designers (including myself) to come up with new collections drawing on Pouenat's unique expertise. I especially love the lamps, by François Champsaur and Damien Langlois-Meurinne in particular.

22 bis passage Dauphine,
75006 Paris
Tel. + 33 (0) 1 43 26 71 49
www.pouenat.fr

Le bazar de l'électricité

This aptly named institution sells bulbs, lamp sockets, and electric leads (including old-fashioned styles in woven sheaths), remade to contemporary standards. There's a workshop, too, where they will rewire lamps and chandeliers, including large models.

34 boulevard Henri-IV, 75004 Paris
Tel. + 33 (0) 1 48 87 83 35
www.bazardelectricite.fr

LAMPSHADES

Carvay

Renald Plessis makes perfect, tasteful lampshades, as well as dispensing expert advice on the best shapes for your vintage lamp-bases picked up at the flea market or thrift store.

33 rue de Bellechasse, 75007 Paris
Tel. + 33 (0) 1 45 33 71 72

PICTURE FRAMES

Prodiver

This small firm works for several top hotels. I often ask the owner, Monsieur Barda, to mount my collection of art photographs on metal: this is the best way to preserve them.

15 rue des Grands-Prés,
92000 Nanterre
Tel. + 33 (0) 1 47 21 32 15

Maison Samson

A neighborhood frame shop, specializing in old and antique frames. They will also make contemporary frames to order.

29 rue Saint-Dominique,
75007 Paris
Tel. + 33 (0) 1 45 51 52 34

SOFT FURNISHINGS

Joyce Pons de Vier

Joyce Pons de Vier has a shop in the Galerie Vivienne (behind the Palais Royal), and makes most of my curtains.

64 galerie Vivienne, 75002 Paris
Tel. + 33 (0) 1 42 96 32 18

Home Sails

An upscale textile firm, making curtains to measure for windows and conservatories. They have a great range of curtain rods, too, in a variety of metal finishes, with ingenious attachments.

178 rue de Charenton, 75012 Paris
Tel. + 33 (0) 1 43 46 54 54
www.homesails.fr

TABLEWARE AND HOUSEHOLD LINENS

Muriel Grateau

Muriel Grateau's recently renovated showroom presents her unique collection of colorful ceramics.

37 rue de Beaune, 75007 Paris
Tel. + 33 1 40 20 42 82
www.murielgrateau.com

Bernardaud

Classic and contemporary collections, by artists and designers. This distinguished porcelain house has embraced modernity while losing none of its proud heritage and essential spirit. I've designed several items for them, including the Prime Time tray and Kirikou tealights.

11 rue Royale, 75001 Paris
Tel. + 33 (0) 1 47 42 82 66
www.bernardaud.fr

ACCESSORIES

Muji

An essential address for well planned storage and decorative accessories. I use their drawers in my bathroom, and their lovely wastebaskets in my offices.

27 rue Saint-Sulpice, 75006 Paris
Tel. + 33 1 44 07 37 30
www.muji.fr

Bath Bazaar

For bathroom mats, toilet-paper holders, magnifying make-up mirrors, and small bathroom wastebaskets.

6 avenue du Maine, 75014 Paris
Tel. + 33 (0) 1 45 48 89 00
www.bathbazaar.fr

ARTISTS' MATERIALS

If you're planning to give your lampshades the gouache treatment, or decorate them with felt-tips and colored crayons, here's where to go for the very best range of colors. My choice for paper, crayons, and Rotring pens.

Sennelier

3 quai Voltaire, 75007 Paris
Tel. + 33 (0) 1 42 60 72 15
www.magasinsennelier.com

Rougier & Plé

108 boulevard Saint-Germain, 75006 Paris
Tel. + 33 (0) 1 56 81 18 35
www.rougier-ple.fr

FLORISTS

Truffaut

For a vast selection of green plants, especially my favorite *Ficus elastica* and *Philodendron monstera deliciosa*.
85 quai de la Gare, 75013 Paris
Tel. + 33 (0) 1 53 60 84 50
www.truffaut.com

Moulié

Naturally, for a quality florist on the place du Palais-Bourbon, Moulié has been supplying French ministries, Paris embassies, and leading couture houses for decades. A classic address in every sense.
8 place du Palais-Bourbon, 75007 Paris
Tel. + 33 (0) 1 45 51 78 43
www.mouliefleurs.com

FURNITURE

India Mahdavi
Mobilier

Opened in 2003, the showroom presents my collection of furniture, made to measure by French artisans. You'll find my ceramic Bishop stools, Bluff coffee table, and Big Swing lamp—and much more!
3 rue Las Cases, 75007 Paris
Tel. + 33 (0) 1 45 55 67 67

Accessoires

Along the same street, at no. 19, a second shop is devoted to my collection of small, stylish objects for the home: cushions, throws, lamps, chairs, and occasional tables, crafted all over the world. Some items are co-productions, with Maison Drucker or ceramicists Jars and Atelier Buffile.
19 rue Las Cases, 75007 Paris
Tel. + 33 (0) 1 45 55 88 88
www.india-mahdavi.com

Silvera

An essential furniture showroom, with a vast selection of work by international designers.
47 rue de l'Université, 75007 Paris
Tel. + 33 (0) 1 45 48 21 06
www.silvera.fr

Maison Darré

India Mahdavi

Galerie Perimeter

Established by Pascal Revert, this upstairs space resembles a private apartment, selling a selection of historic twentieth-century and contemporary furniture, including exclusive limited editions by Janette Laverrière and Adrien Gardère.
47, rue Saint-André-des-Arts, 75006 Paris
Tel. + 33 (0) 1 55 42 01 22
www.perimeter-artanddesign.com

Maison Darré

Vincent Darré's creations have a unique, delightfully baroque, surrealist touch. I love his wallpapers and decorated tabletops, and his wacky approach!
32 rue du Mont-Thabor, Paris 75001
Tel. + 33 (0) 1 42 60 27 97
www.maisondarre.com

Damien Tison

I often drop in to this fabulous little antiques shop. Owners Martial Giraudeau and Damien Tison present a well-chosen range of furniture, lamps, and curios from every period.
75 rue du Cherche-Midi, 75006 Paris
Tel. + 33 (0) 6 61 12 50 53
www.damientison.com

Allt

Didier Maréchal and Charlotte de Martignac visit Denmark and Sweden monthly, in search of Scandinavian objects and furniture from the 1950s to the present. They offer a particularly wide choice, including plastic tableware, vintage cushions, lamps, mirrors, and (of course) furniture of all kinds, at very reasonable prices.
21 rue Lebon, 75012 Paris
Tel. + 33 (0) 6 81 00 00 55
www.allt.fr

Patrick Seguin

Kreo

FURNITURE GALLERIES

Patrick Seguin

Patrick Seguin's loft showroom near
the Bastille presents furniture by Pierre
Jeanneret and Charlotte Perriand, and
architectural designs by Jean Prouvé,
including the Maison des Jours
Meilleurs. A must.
5 rue des Taillandiers, Paris 75011
Tel. + 33 (0) 1 47 00 32 35
www.patrickseguin.com

Equally unmissable, the famous
Carré Rive Gauche
(www.carrerivegauche.com) is home
to antiques dealers on rue de Lille and
rue de Beaune, and furniture galleries
on rue de Seine, rue Dauphine, rue
des Beaux-Arts, and rue Mazarine.
Here are my favorites:

Jacques Lacoste
For furniture by Jean Royère.
12 rue de Seine, 75006 Paris
Tel. + 33 (0) 1 40 20 41 82

Kreo
For new limited editions by
contemporary designers like the
Bouroullec brothers or Martin Szekely.
31 rue Dauphine, 75006 Paris
Tel. + 33 (0) 1 53 10 23 00
www.galeriekreo.com

Galerie Yves Gastou
For a great selection of 1970s chic.
12 rue Bonaparte, 75006 Paris
Tel. + 33 (0) 1 53 73 00 10
www.galerieyvesgastou.com

Galerie Jousse
For furniture by Maria Pergay and
Pierre Paulin, among others.
18 rue de Seine, 75006 Paris
Tel. + 33 (0) 1 53 82 13 60

DownTown
For furniture by Charlotte Perriand,
Jean Prouvé, and Ron Arad, and
sculpture by Takis.
18 and 33 rue de Seine, 75006 Paris
Tel. + 33 (0) 1 46 33 82 41
www.galeriedowntown.com

LES PUCES DE SAINT-OUEN

**The Paris flea market,
rue des Rosiers,
93400 Saint-Ouen**

Benjamin Baillon—Galerie Brasilia

Benjamin Baillon presents a well-chosen mix of sculptures, paintings, and twentieth-century furniture with its finger on the contemporary style pulse.

Marché Paul Bert, allée 2, stand 143
and Marché Serpette, allée 6,
stand 16–17
Tel. + 33 (0)6 17 21 73 46

Dominique Ilous

For a fine selection of striking objects and signed furniture.

Marché Paul Bert, allée 7,
stand 409–411
Tel. + 33 (0)6 11 86 82 37

Maison Jaune

Attractive selection of furniture from the 1950s and 1960s.

Marché Paul Bert, allée 3, stand 145
www.maisonjaune.tumblr.com

James

A passionate collector of work by Brazilian designers: Oscar Niemeyer, Sergio Rodrigues, Jorge Zalszupin—they're all here.

Marché Serpette, allée 4, stand 17–19
Tel. + 33 (0)6 27 49 51 69
www.james-paris.com

Le 7 Paul Bert

This brand-new space has been opened by Francis Holder, owner of the celebrated Ladurée tea shops, who is also a noted art lover and collector.

Here, he offers a fine selection of twentieth-century furniture.

Marché Paul Bert, allée 7
Tel. + 33 (0)6 85 41 35 89

Fragile

Recent arrivals to the market, just next to the Marché Paul Bert, two Milanese collectors present superb Italian furniture from the 1950s to the 1970s.

5 impasse Simon, 93400 Saint-Ouen
Tel. + 39 34 88 92 69 77
www.fragileparis.fr

Guilhem Faget

An interesting address for French furniture, with work by Jean-René Caillette and Charlotte Perriand, displayed in wonderful "sets."

Marché Serpette, allée 6, stand 11
110 rue des Rosiers
Tel. + 33 6 98 03 11 22
www.guilhemfaget.com

If you're strolling around Paris, don't forget:

Hôtel Thoumieux Restaurant Jean-François Piège

79 rue Saint-Dominique,
75007 Paris
Tel. + 33 (0) 1 47 05 49 75
www.thoumieux.fr

Café Germain

25–27 rue de Buci, 75006 Paris
Tel. + 33 (0) 1 43 26 02 93
And in the basement:

Cinéma Paradisio

25–27 rue de Buci, 75006 Paris
www.legermainparadisio.com

rio de janeiro

Galeria Graphos

Pé de Boi

Shopping Siqueira Campos

This antiques mall is a *carioca* version of Paris's Louvre des Antiquaires. Weave your way through the labyrinth to the Galeria Graphos, for an excellent selection of vintage furniture and work by contemporary artists like Vik Muniz.

Galeria Graphos

Rua Siqueira Campos 143
Sobrelojas 01/02, Copacabana,
Rio de Janeiro
Tel. + 55 (21) 2255 8283

Pé de Boi

The no. 1 boutique for artisan crafts from the four corners of Brazil.
I love their *capim dourado* table sets, made from dried grasses with a soft, golden sheen.
Rua Ipiranga 55, Laranjeiras,
Rio de Janeiro, 22231-120
Tel. + 55 (21) 2285 4395
www.pedeboi.com.br

A Cena Muda

A delightful green and blue kiosk in Ipanema, selling hidden treasures. I adore their old postcards, photograph albums, and decoration magazines (*Domus, Design Interiors, Abitare*) from the 1970s and 1980s.
Rua Visconde de Pirajà 54,
Ipanema, Rio de Janeiro
Tel. + 55 (21) 2287 8072

Rio Scenarium

Mercado Moderno

Santo Scenarium

Whenever I'm in Rio on the first
Saturday of the month, I head for
the street antiques fair on Rua
do Lavradio, followed by a lunch
of *feijoada* at Santo Scenarium,
surrounded by carved saints and holy
reliquaries—the essence of Rio.
**Rua do Lavradio 36, Centro Antigo,
Rio de Janeiro
Tel. + 55 (21) 3147 9007**

Rio Scenarium

A renovated warehouse full of crazy
finds and decor over three stories,
and, above all, *the* party place in Rio
right now.
**Rua do Lavradio 20, Centro Antigo,
Rio de Janeiro
Tel. + 55 (21) 3147 9005
www.rioscenarium.com.br**

Mercado Moderno

Marcelo Vasconcellos was one of the
first dealers to rediscover furniture by
the great Brazilian architect-designers
of the 1940s, '50s, and '60s, like
Joaquim Tenreiro, Sergio Rodrigues,
or Jorge Zalszupin, which is why his
shop is one of my favorite addresses.
Other stops along the same street
include a line-up of cluttered antiques
emporia (especially Sergio Menezes),
great for attractive, unexpected finds.
**Rua do Lavradio 130, Lapa,
Rio de Janeiro
Tel. + 55 (21) 2508 6083**

Confeitaria Colombo

Jardim Botânico

Jardim Botânico

Rio's vast botanic gardens are a must
for the majestic avenue of imperial
palms (the ultimate graphic motif),
the exotic flowers unrivaled anywhere
else, and the outsize waterlilies.
A great place to get lost!
**Rua Jardim Botânico 1008,
Rio de Janeiro
Tel. + 55 (21) 3874 1808
www.jbrj.gov.br**

Confeitaria Colombo

I love the coconut cakes in this über-
cult *carioca* tearoom. Like savoring a
Mont Blanc *chez* Angelina on Paris's
rue de Rivoli (but the XXL version).
**Rua Gonçalves Dias 32, Centro,
Rio de Janeiro
Tel. + 55 (21) 2505 1500
www.confeitariacolombo.com.br**

Aprazivel

Instituto Moreira Salles

Museu de Arte Contemporânea

Quite simply one of the most spectacular buildings by the late master of Brazilian architecture Oscar Niemeyer.

Mirante da Boa Viagem, Niterói,
Rio de Janeiro, 24210-390
Tel. + 55 (21) 2620 2400
www.macniteroi.com.br

Aprazivel

A corner of paradise, in a secluded, natural setting on the slopes of Santa Teresa. If not for the view over the Bay of Rio, you'd think you were in the depths of the jungle. Don't miss their hearts of palm, which are absolutely delicious.

Rua Aprazivel 62, Santa Teresa,
Rio de Janeiro
Tel. + 55 (21) 2508 9174
www.aprazivel.com.br

Instituto Moreira Salles

A 1940s house by Olavo Redig de Campos, one of the great figures of modern architecture, with gardens by the wonderful Roberto Burle Marx— the inventor of tropical landscaped gardens and the man behind Copacabana's famous black-and-white paving stones. The Institut presents excellent temporary exhibitions, too. A gem, far from the hustle and bustle of the city.

Rua Marquês de São Vicente 476,
Gávea, Rio de Janeiro, 22451-040
Tel. + 55 (21) 3284 7400
www.ims.com.br

my favorite online addresses

BLOGS

A great way to keep up with the latest trends, recent projects, and cultural happenings.

Architecture and design

For architecture news:
www.dezeen.com
www.sleekdesign.fr (site in English and French)
www.muuuz.com
www.contemporist.com
www.design-milk.com

If you don't happen to have a complete set of *Domus*, from Taschen, you can follow the latest architecture news from the magazine's international correspondents, at www.domusweb.it

Culture

Art publisher Phaidon's website offers a rich selection of events and publications on the international art, architecture, and culinary scenes:
www.phaidon.com/agenda

Dispatches from *New York Times* correspondents worldwide:
tmagazine.blogs.nytimes.com

This plain, understated website by New York graphic designers Pentagram invites guest designers and architects—from Ronan Bouroullec to Shigeru Ban and Milton Glaser—to share their favorite books:
www.designersandbooks.com

Lifestyle

For the latest news:
www.designboom.com/eng
www.yatzer.com
www.thecoolhunter.net

This site combines decoration addresses worldwide with tips for your own DIY projects back at home:
www.designsponge.com

This site captures the essence of simple Scandinavian design, presented by a dedicated blogger sharing her favorite interior decoration discoveries from around the world:
www.emmas.blogg.se

For miscellaneous interiors and great ideas:
www.style-files.com

DATABASE

Furniture

These fabulous search portals cover all periods and genres, for furniture, fashion, jewelry, and books:
www.1stdibs.com
www.deconet.com

Materials

Practical websites listing everything from materials suppliers to galleries:
www.architonic.com/fr
www.archiexpo.fr

E-SHOPPING

Anthropologie is a cult NY address whose complete collections are accessible online. Among my favorite things are their customized retro handles, and their well-chosen selection of kilims:
www.anthropologie.eu

At the MoMA Design Store, you'll find a selection of art books and everyday objects by leading designers:
www.momastore.org

For fun and successful picture displays at home, here are two sites offering art photographs and original prints at reasonable prices. They will also frame and deliver:
www.20x200.com
www.wantedparis.com

A perfect solution for Moms-in-a-hurry, looking for pretty things for their kids' birthday parties. International shipping is possible. A welcome touch of poetry and simplicity; the blog is delightful and inspirational, too:
www.mylittleday.fr
mylittleday.fr/blog

Check out the capsule collections in France's top catalogs, for great, affordable design ideas:
www.3suisses.com
www.laredoute.com

Coming soon, my very own e-shop in 2013!

. . . and **Siwa**

Simply the most beautiful place on Earth: the Adrère Amellal eco-lodge at **Sidi al-Ja'afar, Siwa Oasis, Siwa, Egypt** **www.adrereamellal.net**

notes

notes

notes

notes

notes

acknowledgments

warmest thanks to
Teresa Cremisi for her generosity and concern; Julie Rouart for her energy
and patience; Noémie Levain for her rigorous attention to detail; Erik Emptaz,
my first (male) reader, and his unfailing sense of humor; Violaine Binet,
my first (female) reader, and her eagle eye.

and also
Everyone in my team, especially Tala, Apolline, Virginie, Charlotte, Karine,
and Marie, for their invaluable help, without which I would never have been
able to deliver this "homemade" book on time; Derek Hudson, the official
photographer of all "my" homes; Capucine Puerari for her instinctive,
unerring eye; Hervé Bourgeois and Guillaume Richard for a highly productive
two-and-three-quarter-hour journey aboard the Eurostar; and Carlos Couturier
and Murat Suter for their active contributions to the city guide.

All of my clients—willing victims of my golden rules and quick tips—thanks
to whom I have decorated (among others) the Hôtel du Cloître, the Jean-François
Piège restaurant and the Hôtel Thoumieux, Claridge's, the Germain Paradisio,
the Monte-Carlo Beach, the Connaught, the Condesa df, the Townhouse....
All the artisans and businesses, both big and small, and all the painters, cabinet-
makers, marble-cutters, staff masons, builders, electricians, and plumbers
who have collaborated on my projects since the beginning.

All of my friends, whose homes are so often the setting for my impromptu-style
consultations.

And as always, forever, my mother, my father, and Miles.
india

a thousand thanks to
Anne-Cécile Sarfati, to whom I first mentioned this project, and who supported
it from the outset.

Sylvie de Chirée, Catherine Scotto, and Catherine Roig, high priestesses
of home decoration for *Elle Décoration* and *Elle*. This book came about partly
thanks to their confidence in my work, my interviews with India on a host of
subjects, and the many other projects I have undertaken for them.

My daughters Antonia and Lucie (and their dad), for being so lovely,
understanding, and patient, even in "stormy weather."
soline

illustration captions

p. 20 Studio chair by Makkink & Bey
p. 22 Photograph by Jean-Michel Aucler
p. 23 "L-R Bookshelf" picture by Isidro Blasco
pp. 24–25 Photograph by Derek Hudson
p. 26 Photograph by Derek Hudson
p. 27 Drawing by Rupert Shrive
Paper lampshade by David Hicks
Console and Bishop stool/side table by
India Mahdavi
pp. 28–29 Lamp by P. Henningsen
Photograph by Jean-Michel Aucler
p. 32 Furniture by India Mahdavi
Wall light by .PSLAB
p. 34 Vintage armchair, cushions,
and small objects by India Mahdavi
p. 36 Chairs by Hans Wegner
p. 40 Set of chairs by Maarten Baas
Table by Fabiaan Van Severen
Sofa by India Mahdavi
Coffee table by Takis
pp. 44–45 left: Sculpture by Jeff Koons
center: Wall sculpture by Franz West
Chairs by Hans Wegner
Ottoman by Christian Astuguevieille
right: Sculpture by Xavier Veilhan
pp. 46–47 left: Vintage table and bench
Chairs by Hans Wegner
Lamp by India Mahdavi
Drawing by Adel Abdessemed
right: Reservoir Dog bookshelf
by India Mahdavi
Vintage wall lamp
pp. 48–49 Bishop stools/side tables
by India Mahdavi
Vintage yellow three-piece suite
Vintage orange armchair
Coffee tables by Hubert le Gall,
India Mahdavi, Gio Ponti
pp. 50–51 left: Chaise longue by
Jean Prouvé
Bishop stool/side table by India Mahdavi
Standard lamp by Florence Lopez (reissued)
Photograph by Derek Hudson
right: Ringo side table by India Mahdavi
Smoking No Smoking ashtrays by India
Mahdavi
pp. 52–53 left: Wooden bench seat
by India Mahdavi, Vintage table

right: Vintage lamp (paper shade by David
Hicks)
Stools by Christian Astuguevieille
Bishop stool/side table by India Mahdavi
Vintage armchair and table
Cushion by India Mahdavi's brand
Petits Objets
Bernardaud vase
Drawing by Rupert Shrive
Photograph by Alex Prager
pp. 54–55 Set of chairs by
Florian Borkenhagen
Charpin mirror
pp. 56–57 Leather ceiling lamp by Frères
Bouroullec
Furniture group by India Mahdavi
Cushions by Lindell
Throw by India Mahdavi
pp. 58–59 left: Furniture group by India
Mahdavi
Cushions by Lindell
Throw, bedside lamps, Bishop stool/side
table by India Mahdavi
right: Armchair by India Mahdavi
Lamp by India Mahdavi
Ceiling light by Frères Bouroullec
Chair by Studio Makkink & Bey
pp. 60–61 Straw coat stand by Gervasoni
Bed and ottoman by India Mahdavi
pp. 62–63 left: Table by Martino Gamper
Set of chairs by Cherner
right: Chairs by Maarten Baas
Ceiling lamp by Verner Pantone
Table by India Mahdavi
pp. 64–65 right: Customized lamp
by Christian Liaigre
Invitation from Irving Penn
right: Photograph by Aurore de la Morinerie
pp. 66–67 Set of chairs by Franz West
Double Diagonal table by India Mahdavi
Accessories and small objects by India
Mahdavi
pp. 68–69 Foufoune fun-fur ottoman by
India Mahdavi
right: Sculpture by Lamberto Correggiari
p. 70 Mirror by India Mahdavi
Cupboard handles by India Mahdavi
Wall light by .PSLAB

p. 71 Ceiling light by Foc, customized by India Mahdavi
p. 72 Collaboration with GBRH
p. 79 Lamp by India Mahdavi
Vintage bench
Drawing by Adel Abdessemed
pp. 80–81 Portrait medallions by Julian Opie
Star table by India Mahdavi
Ottomans and table by India Mahdavi
Fitted carpet by Tai Ping
Vintage armchairs
pp. 82–83 Carpet by Manufacture de Cogolin
Wall lamps by .PSLAB
Ceiling lamp by Frères Bouroullec, Galerie Kreo, Paris
Screen by Zoé Ouvrier
Zebra skins and stuffed peacock by Deyrolle
Embroidered leopardskin by Lindell
Furniture by India Mahdavi
pp. 84–85 Four-poster bed by Maria Pergay
Bishop bedside tables by India Mahdavi
Vintage lamp
Fitted carpet by India Mahdavi
pp. 90–91 Sculpture by Xavier Veilhan
Furniture by India Mahdavi
p. 93 Sculpture by Xavier Veilhan
Furniture by India Mahdavi
p. 95 Furniture by India Mahdavi
pp. 96–97 Armchair by India Mahdavi
Throw by Lindell
Bedside lamps by Arne Jacobsen, La Maison du Danemark
p. 99 Washbasins by India Mahdavi
p. 101 Sofa and cushions by India Mahdavi
Screen by India Mahdavi
Photograph by Marc le Mené
p. 102 Bedside lamp by Arne Jacobsen, La Maison du Danemark
Screen and Bishop stool/side table by India Mahdavi
p. 103 Photograph by Aurore de la Morinerie
Armchair by Don Carlos
Lollipop lamp by India Mahdavi

p. 105 IKEA desk
Sculpture by Rupert Shrive
Photograph by Jean Noël de Soye
p. 106 Furniture by IKEA
Cushions by India Mahdavi
Photograph by Jean Noël de Soye
Photograph by Yuki Onodera
p. 107 Furniture by IKEA
Photograph by Jean Noël de Soye
p. 110 (01) India Mahdavi showroom
(02) Coffee table by Gio Ponti
(03) Coffee table by De Padova
(04) Coffee table by India Mahdavi
(05) Coffee table by India Mahdavi
p. 112 (04) Wall light and coffee tables by India Mahdavi
p. 116 (01) Sofa by India Mahdavi
Fan by Maarten Baas
Standard lamp by India Mahdavi
(02, top to bottom)
Wall lights by India Mahdavi
Wall lights by M/M Paris
(03) Armchair by Arne Jacobsen
Table by India Mahdavi
Vintage three-branched standard lamp
p. 118 Diagonal table by India Mahdavi
Vintage lamps
p. 120 (02) Throw by India Mahdavi
(05) Loops rug by India Mahdavi
p. 125 Cushions and small objects by India Mahdavi
Vintage lamp
p. 127 Lamp by India Mahdavi
pp. 130–131 Embroidered leopardskin by Lindell
Cushions by Lindell
p. 134 Bamboo armchairs by Albini
Cushions by Lindell
Plants from Moulié
p. 137 Ashtrays by India Mahdavi
p. 139 Cupboard by India Mahdavi
p. 141 Customized portrait

photographic credits

Illustrations by India Mahdavi
pp. 8, 10, 12, 14, 18, 30, 42, 76, 108, 122, 132, 142
Studio imh pp. 16, 32, 40, 44, 54, 73, 74, 88, 89, 91, 94, 95, 99, 101, 102, 116, 120, 130, 131, 141, 164, 165
Derek Hudson pp. 21, 26, 27, 28, 29, 34, 36, 44, 45, 46, 47, 48, 49, 51, 53, 55, 56, 58, 59, 62, 63, 64, 65, 66, 68, 69, 70, 75, 79, 90, 91, 93, 96, 97, 100, 110, 112, 114, 120, 139
Jean-François Jaussaud/Lux Productions
pp. 23, 24, 25, 50, 52, 82, 83, 84, 85, 87, 125, 129, 135
Condesa DF p. 57
Thierry Bouët pp. 60, 61
Sanam Gharagozlou pp. 67, 112
Béatrice Amagat p. 71
Pierre Paradis p. 72
Dick Liu p. 73
Philippe Chancel p. 103
Vincent Ferrane/Elle/Scoop
pp. 105, 106, 107
Todd McPhail p. 112
Jean-Jacques L'Héritier p. 112
Émilie Erbin p. 116
Vincent Leroux p. 116
Thierry Depagne pp. 116, 136
François de Font-Réaulx p. 118
Nicolas Tosi/Elle Décoration/Scoop
pp. 144 right, 145 left, 146 left
Agop Kanledjian p. 145 right
François Gâté/ Elle Décoration/Scoop
p. 149 right
Nicolas Mathéus/Elle Décoration/Scoop
pp. 156, 157, 166 right, 169 left
Marc Dantan p. 178 right
Frédéric Vasseur/ Elle Décoration/Scoop
pp. 186 right, 188 right
Paulo Rodrigues p. 187 right
Rogério Van Krüger p. 188 left